The Internet
For Genealogists:
A Beginner's Guide

The Internet For Genealogists: A Beginner's Guide

By Barbara Renick and Richard S. Wilson

Published by:
Compuology
330 La Serna Avenue
La Habra, CA 90631-2801
Phone: 562/690-5588
E-mail: sales@compuology.com

Distributed to the trade by Betterway Books
an imprint of F & W Publications, Inc.
1507 Dana Avenue
Cincinnati, OH 45207
1-800/289-0963

First printing, July 1998
10 9 8 7 6 5 4 3 2

Printed in the United States of America.

ISBN 0-938717-41-3

About the Authors

Barbara Renick

Barbara Renick brings more than thirteen years of online experience to this publication and has been active in genealogical research for more than 25 years. She is an author and contributing editor to the *NGS/CIG Digest*. She is a national and local lecturer on the subjects of the Internet, genealogy, and genealogical computing, and has taught PAF classes since 1985.

Barbara is currently on staff at the LDS Regional Family History Center in Orange, California. She is the secretary and newsletter editor of the Southern California Chapter of the Association of Professional Genealogists. Her memberships include: the National Genealogical Society, the Association of Professional Genealogists, as well as many state and local genealogical societies. Barbara can be reached electronically on the Internet at: **BarbZR@msn.com** or **barbzr@rgenealogy.com**.

Richard S. Wilson

Richard S. Wilson also brings more than fourteen years of online experience to this publication and has been doing genealogical research for more than nineteen years. He is a national and local lecturer on the subjects of the Internet, genealogy, and genealogical computing and has written articles for national magazines, and is the owner of Compuology–a genealogical-based computer company (**http://www.compuology.com**). Richard received his Bachelors Degree from the California State University, Long Beach and taught a monthly Computer Interest Group for the Whittier Area Genealogy Society (WAGS) from 1992 to 1997.

Richard is the state coordinator for the California USGenWeb Project on the Internet and is president of the Southern California Chapter of the Association of Professional Genealogists. He has memberships in the National Genealogical Society, the Association of Professional Genealogists, the California State Genealogical Alliance, a life membership in the Whittier Area Genealogy Society, as well as many local genealogical societies. Richard's Internet address is: **wilson@compuology.com**.

Acknowledgments

Many people have assisted us in getting our book completed and in its final form. We would first like to thank all of the people who insisted a book like this was needed, and prompted us to take the time to write it. A special thanks goes to those who assisted with proofreading the initial drafts of the book.

We would like to thank Craig Roberts Scott, MA, CGRS, FSA Scot, for his time and important feedback in the development of this book. Another thanks goes to George Archer for his comments, ideas and suggestions.

Lastly, we would like to thank Dr. Gary Shumway of the History Department at California State University, Fullerton for his additional advice and help getting the initial versions of our book published.

Table of Contents

Part I: Understanding the Internet 1
    In the Beginning 3
    Why Genealogists Love the Internet 7
    Merging Onto the Information Superhighway 14

Part II: Getting Online 19
    Web Browsers 21
    Using E-mail Software 22
    Mail Lists 27
    Newsgroups 36
    Chat Sessions 42
    Netiquette 43
    FTP - What is it? Do I have it? 44
    Surfing vs. Searching the Internet 48

Part III: Internet Resources for Genealogists 61
    General Genealogy Sites 64
    Netiquette 67
    Genealogy Megasites 68
    Ethnic and Special Interest Sites 72
    Foreign Genealogy Research Sites 76
    Language Aids 81
    Genealogical Software Sites 83
    Genealogical and Historical Societies Online 90
    Library & Catalog Sites 98
    Map & Gazetteer Sites 102
    Genealogy Book Stores & Publishers 106
    Online Genealogy Publications 112
    Online Databases for Genealogists 114
    Genealogy Tools & Training 131
    Citing Sources & Writing Skills 142
    Copyright Information 143

Mail Lists, Newsgroups, & Chat Sites 144
Locating Living People 146
Other Computer Software Sites 149
Internet Search Tools 152
Genealogy Graphics Sites 158
E-mail Services 160
Travel Services 162

Part IV: Where Do We Go Next? 165
Where Is the Internet Headed? 167
What Effect Will Internet Growth
        Have on Genealogy? 168

Appendix A: Choosing an ISP 169
Important Considerations 171
Internet Service Providers: Local & National 173
Telnet Access 174

Appendix B: Glossary 175

Index 197

Symbols Used in This Book

Technical Note

Warning

Tip

This book is primarily written for genealogists with access to computers that can use a graphical interface: Windows 3.x, Windows 95/98 or the Macintosh operating systems.

If you run into words you don't understand while reading this book please check in the glossary located at the back of the book starting on page 177.

Part I: Understanding the Internet

In the Beginning

The Internet is a vast resource for genealogists today. However, the Internet was not originally created as a genealogical tool. At its inception, the Internet was not intended to be a public tool at all.

The Bible tells us God created the earth in six days. It took the U.S. government a little longer to create the Internet. This also explains why the Internet languished for several decades. The Internet did not become popular until the business community (and a couple of graduate students) improved upon it.

There is a good reason why the Internet remained the playground of government rocket scientists, university professors, and brain surgeons for so many years. This is because the U.S. government originally built the Internet around Telnet protocols. Telnet is an ugly, arcane, text-based computer language. It did, and still does, let your computer talk to other computers around the world, but at what a price!

```
                      (Typical Telnet Session)
06/21/97          SELECTED DATABASE:  LAPL PAC              09:47 P.M

             THE COMPUTER CAN FIND ITEMS BY:

                    NAME (AUTHORS)    =  NB
                    TITLE             =  T
                    SUBJECT           =  SB
                    WORD              =  W
                    PATRON INFORMATION=  PI

GO AHEAD! TYPE THE LETTER(S) (NB, T, SB, W or PI ) FOR THE KIND OF
     SEARCH YOU WANT AND PRESS <RETURN>.

          FOR ADDITIONAL AND QUICK WAYS TO SEARCH, TYPE QS

            FOR HELP, TYPE ? AT ANY POINT IN YOUR SEARCH
               OR FOR A COMPLETE HELP MENU, TYPE ?H

     ENTER  COMMAND  >>
```

The example on the previous page is a Telnet session to the Los Angeles Public Library's online catalog. As you can see from the example, a Telnet session can be rather hard to understand. Telnet commands (like DOS computer commands) are often cryptic.

During a Telnet session, it is not uncommon to have to work through several layers of computer languages. Each Telnet site has its own set of commands and often each database at a site will have its own unique commands as well. This makes it confusing to know which set of commands to use next or even to remember the different commands to exit each layer. Any of the following commands might be used to exit the Telnet system you are stuck in: //**exit** or **exi** or **g** or **bye** or **logoff**.

In a worst case scenario if you are stuck, you can always turn off your modem (if it is an external modem) or close down the communications program on your computer. If you do this, you risk leaving fractured files at both ends (on your computer and the computer you were logged onto).

The only reason genealogists need to know about Telnet is because a few older sites on the Internet, especially some large library catalogs, are still only accessible and searchable via Telnet. Fortunately this is becoming less common as the Internet matures.

It wasn't until the World Wide Web came along, just a few years ago, that the Internet became a popular public forum. One day, two graduate students became fed up with the ugly Telnet system they had to use to access the Internet. They developed an easy-to-use point and click interface. This interface solved many of the navigational problems inherent in the old Telnet system. This interface became the World Wide Web (WWW or "The Web") that we have today.

The Internet began as a U.S. military experiment called ARPAnet over 20 years ago. At that time, more and more aspects of national defense were relying on computers. Fears of a nuclear war were high, thus the decision was made to create a computer network that would still operate and relay commands, even if many segments or nodes were knocked out by a man-made or natural disaster. In such a fault-tolerant network, a computer in Kansas City could be destroyed without cutting off communications between Washington DC and Los Angeles.

At the same time that ARPAnet was being developed, academic researchers were increasing their use of computers. Some of the problems they were tackling required access to the most powerful computers in the world. Arrangements were made to give non-military users access to a handful of supercomputers via the Internet, as it existed then. The ARPAnet was dismantled and a more powerful network, called NSFNET, was put in its place.

The National Science Foundation was responsible for the NSFNET. Five supercomputers were installed at various locations around the country. A network was designed and built which connected universities to each other and to the supercomputer centers. In order for a university or college to be connected to NSFNET (and have that connection to the Internet be funded by the federal government), that institution was required to provide free Internet access to all of its teachers, students and administrators. At that time, Windows, the Macintosh system, and graphical computer interfaces did not exist (except in experimental environments). This was the beginning of the text-based Internet. Nevertheless, just the ability to send an electronic "letter" to a friend in seconds, or trade text files about research in minutes with someone across the country created a huge demand for Internet access.

The largest contribution to the Internet was made by a few independent computer networking masters. Rather than waiting for the government, these men worked out the protocols (standards) that could be used by any computer to communicate with others, thus making the world wide Internet possible. With the Internet up and running, large companies with national and international computer networks realized that they could better utilize their resources by connecting their computers to the Internet. Thus, the Information Superhighway was born.

The Web was made possible by two developments:

- The evolution of computers to support multimedia as well as text files.

- The development of Web browser software which allows the computer user to "read" or "view" colorful multimedia Web pages and easily navigate from Web page to Web page.

The Internet and the World Wide Web are, therefore, not separate entities. The World Wide Web is merely the youngest part of the Internet. The WWW is the most popular and rapidly growing segment of the Internet today. That is why much of this book focuses on the World Wide Web for genealogists.

Genealogists find two basic types of resources on the Internet:

- Other people (genealogists, archivists, historians, etc.)

- Information (stored anywhere around the world on a computer that is connected to the Internet)

The Internet allows genealogists to do three things:

- Browse pages (both text-based and graphical)

- E-mail (personal and public postings)

- Transfer files (FTP is both text-based and graphical)

These three basic processes can be used in different ways. For example, FTP (see page 44 for more on FTP) can be used to download a software upgrade, but special software programs also use FTP for live, online chat sessions via the typed word. Thus, the different parts of the Internet have many different looks.

The Internet also has many different names, ranging from "the Information Superhighway" to just "the Net." Understanding how and why the Internet was created helps the genealogist understand why there are so many routes to be followed when traveling the Information Superhighway.

Why Genealogists Love the Internet

If there is one thing genealogists love more than cemeteries, it is libraries. <grin> The Internet has been called the world's largest library and with good reason. The Net makes a world of resources available to genealogists twenty-four hours per day at very reasonable costs. Most resources for genealogists on the Internet are free.

Genealogists love the Internet for:

- ♥ finding people (dead or alive)
- ♥ research
- ♥ software
- ♥ education and training
- ♥ travel help
- ♥ language aids
- ♥ finding calendars of genealogy events
- ♥ locating societies (historical and genealogical)
- ♥ purchasing genealogical products and services
- ♥ medical resources
- ♥ social interaction

♥ Finding People (dead or alive)

Finding dead people is what genealogy is all about; however, there are many reasons genealogists may want to find living people. You may want to search for researchers with whom you had contact years before. You may want to find someone who wrote a book about a branch of your family. Additionally, you might be interested in locating long-lost living relatives who may have unique family records to share.

The Internet provides many specialized search services that operate like the White Pages published by your telephone company. Most of these services offer free searches of their databases. Others charge a small fee. Such Internet search services exist for both domestic and foreign areas. They often list individuals who register their e-mail and/or snail mail addresses. You may find yourself listed, even if you have not registered and have an unlisted telephone number. Privacy issues on the Internet are a major concern today.

Other search possibilities include online databases compiled from voter registrations and motor vehicle registrations, which may be searchable for a small fee. The U. S. Social Security Death Index is available for free online searching.

There are innumerable Internet genealogy sites that allow you to place a free query about a person (dead or alive) that you are looking for. All of these different Internet approaches can help you find the people you want to contact. (See the "Locating Living People" section, in *Part III*, starting on page 146).

♥ Research

More and more genealogists are starting to go to the Internet first for help and information (even original sources) before they travel to more traditional research facilities. The Internet brings many research tools right into your home. *PC Magazine* ("Top 100 Web Sites" 18 February 1997) says: "Genealogy is the perfect hobby for the Web; it demands excellent research tools and far-reaching communications."

Genealogists no longer need go out blindly to do research hoping that a library or archive will have something they want to search. With the Internet, you can now (most of the time) look through at least a partial catalog of that institution's holdings before you go there to research.

You are often able to look up the call number and the shelf location of records. Many libraries indicate how many copies of a book they have, and if that book is currently checked out. You may find information about operating hours and locations of copy machines. Sometimes such Web sites even include information about whether you need specific change, paper money, or a copy card for making photocopies of the information you find.

The best finding aids and the most commonly used primary source records are being digitized and placed online. The Library of Virginia is one of the pioneer organizations in this effort. What a delight it is to be able to download at midnight an image of an original Bible record or a 1786 land record surveyed by Daniel Boone.

♥ Software

One of the biggest challenges to genealogical computing is using software. Genealogists suffer through bugs and glitches in the software programs they buy.

Those who go online find a world of resources to help them with the challenges of genealogical computing. Chat areas and e-mail discussion groups on the Internet put you in contact with other genealogists and computer users who have had similar problems and who may have found the solutions to your problems.

Most software companies have Internet Web sites including those companies that produce genealogical software. There genealogists can learn about these products. Many Web sites allow you to download free demonstration versions of their software. Often you can buy and download a full version of the software, saving yourself a trip to the local computer store. Many companies offer free upgrades to their software and technical support online. It is always wise to check a product's Web site before you call them for technical support.

♥ Education and Training

Education and training are the lifeblood of genealogy. Genealogists continuously pursue further knowledge. The Internet can provide you with unparalleled opportunities for training in the techniques and sources for genealogical research – without even leaving your home!

Virtual University classes specifically tailored for genealogists are available. Regular online chat sessions are held for genealogists to share experiences, ideas and concerns. Many Web pages are devoted to tutorials on everything from getting started in genealogy to reading early American handwriting and tracing manuscript sources.

♥ Travel Help

Genealogists love to travel. They want to walk the land their ancestors walked, touch their ancestors' gravestones, and hold in their hands documents written by their ancestors a century ago. Genealogists love to visit cousins and attend genealogical conferences. While you cannot do these things online, the Internet can help you do them more conveniently and with less expense.

There are free services, like Expedia (**http://www.expedia.com/**), and Travelocity (**http://www.travelocity.com/**), that track airfares. Such online services send regular e-mail messages to you with the lowest registered fares to your desired destinations and allow you to purchase airline tickets online.

Many accommodations, from small bed and breakfast inns to large hotel chains, are represented on the World Wide Web. With the Internet, you can make rental car reservations all over the world. It is easy to reserve a rental car in Poland (with or without an English-speaking chauffeur). One Polish car rental Web site even reminds you which documents to bring so you don't encounter difficulties when you arrive.

The Internet takes away your excuses for getting lost while trying to locate a particular address. Free online map sites (such as MapBlast! located at **http://www.mapblast.com/** and MapQuest at **http://www.mapquest.com/** allow you to generate a colorful map of your destination. These services give you the power to zoom in or out to check your route. Some online services even print driving directions from your specified current location to your destination. As with any map service, be prepared to encounter obstacles that may have not yet made their way onto the map database.

The Internet can help with other travel concerns. You can check the weather at your destination before you leave home with The Weather Channel at **http://www.weather.com/**. This site also indicates airport delays at the forty busiest airports in the USA. The Weather Channel includes a Web page where you can check for flight delays, if you know your flight number, via data from Flyte Comm of Florida.

♥ Language Aids

The Internet has a language all its own. The glossary in this book should get you started with this new language. When you become comfortable navigating on the Internet, you will be ready to use sites like PC Webopaedia at **http://www.webopedia.com/** for further help understanding the language of computers and the Internet.

Have you ever found a Web page in a foreign language or received an e-mail message in the language of your ancestors? No problem. The Alta Vista search engine site at **http://altavista.digital.com/** includes a language translation option for such situations. If Alta Vista's foreign language dictionary doesn't have the words you need, go to one of the Web sites like A Web of On-line Dictionaries by R. Beard. This site at **http://www.bucknell.edu/~rbeard/diction.html** includes links to more than 500 dictionaries in more than 140 languages.

There are online dictionaries for special topics too. A free genealogy dictionary is at **http://www.electriciti.com/~dotts/diction.html**. A useful list of occupation names compared in Latin, Polish, and English is at **http://hum.amu.edu.pl/~rafalp/GEN/zawody.htm**. There is even a Web site where you can type a word and the site searches 285 different specialty dictionaries simultaneously (OneLook Dictionaries page at **http://www.onelook.com/**). This site includes legal, medical and scientific dictionaries.

What do you do if it's the middle of the night and you can't read a photocopy of a Tennessee land record you made on your last research trip? If you are on the Internet, you can find a glossary of land terminology at **http://www.tngenweb.org/tnland/terms.htm** to help figure out a word or two. If you don't understand the metes and bounds land system as found in Tennessee land records in the early 1800's, go to a tutorial at **http://www.tngenweb.org/tnland/metes-b.htm**. When it comes down to the root of the matter, you can even find a Web site about the trees mentioned in early land records for Middle Tennessee at **http://www.tngenweb.org/tnland/trees.htm**

♥ Finding Calendars of Genealogical Events

The Internet has calendars of genealogical events held in your area or around the world. Such Web sites often allow you to display lists of events in geographic or chronological order. These Web sites usually include information on how to have your society's genealogical event listed too.

♥ Locating Societies

The local genealogical or historical society in the area where your ancestor lived may be of great help to you in tracing your family tree. Experienced genealogists typically belong to many genealogical and historical societies. They generally belong to one or more societies near their home for the social interaction and educational opportunities. The USGenWeb and World GenWeb Projects make it easy to locate genealogical and historical societies around the world. More and more societies have their own Web sites with useful information.

At these societies' meetings you can mingle, in person, with people who share your passion for genealogy. Genealogists need contact with other genealogists to share their joys and sorrows, research tips and techniques, help and advice.

♥ Purchasing Genealogical Products and Supplies

On the Internet, with a credit card, you can purchase everything from groceries (**http://www.netgrocer.com/**) to an automobile (like a Cadillac at **http://www.autovision.com/r_cad.htm**) to genealogical products and supplies. The Internet often saves you time and money because it allows you to conveniently comparative products and shop from the comfort of your home.

The Internet saves genealogists money in many ways. Free reference tools are available twenty-four hours a day from around the world. These include dictionaries, databases, translation services, and tutorials, to name a few. Such reference tools, if purchased in CD or book form, not only cost money but also immediately become dated, collect dust, and take up valuable shelf space.

♥ Medical Resources

Many people begin researching their family trees for medical reasons. There are Web sites that offer free medical advice, just as there are many Web sites and e-mail discussion groups that offer free genealogical advice.

You need to realize the expertise of online sources varies. Carefully evaluate the information you receive. Just because it's in print, whether in a book or on the Web, doesn't make it true. However, the Internet gives you an up-to-date place to start your medical and/or genealogical research.

Barbara Says:

My husband recommended that I search for a "Genealogist's Anonymous" site. Instead, I made a pact with him not to do genealogy after 5:00 p.m. However, he didn't say anything about 5:00 a.m. You will often find less congestion on the Information Superhighway at that time of day. <grin>

♥ Social Interaction

For some reason, your family and regular friends often fail to appreciate your stories of genealogical trials and triumphs. It takes another genealogist to understand just what you have been experiencing. Mail lists and newsgroups on the Internet give you a way to share your triumphs without leaving home. These feelings are also giving impetus to live Chat rooms and Chat sessions on the Internet.

Chat rooms bring the genealogy community into your own home. This is convenient for those who find it difficult to participate at more conventional genealogical gatherings.

Barbara Says:

Some people fear going online because they feel their computer will be infected with a computer virus. Richard and I have a total of twenty-seven years online and neither of us ever had our computers infected in this manner. The most common ways to catch a computer virus are: children carrying it home from their friend's computer when they "share" games, or from a brand new computer program disk (floppy or CD-ROM). This means you still need to make backups frequently and use virus detection software whether you are online or not.

Merging Onto the Information Superhighway

The Internet is nothing more than a collection of computers and computer networks. It allows everything from a single computer to a network of computers to a large mainframe computer to communicate with each other and exchange information. The basic principle of the Internet is the client-server relationship. You and your computer are the client and your Internet Service Provider's computer is the server. Unless your computer is connected to a server (or is a server), it cannot communicate with other computers on the Internet.

Our public telephone system works in a similar way. Your telephone functions like the client in a client-server relationship. The phone company's switch box is the server. When you make a telephone call, your call goes to the local phone company's central office. From there, a switch routes your call from one switching box to another. Eventually your call reaches a phone company switching box that can connect you to the telephone of the person you are calling. You cannot call someone else's telephone directly. Without the phone company, your telephone could not reach anyone else's telephone. Similarly, without an Internet Service Provider (ISP) you cannot connect to other computers on the Internet.

You, the genealogist, connect to the Internet via a computer and modem, which allow you to send and receive information over a standard telephone line. When your computer dials into your ISP, it is like making that first connection to the local phone company's central switching box, except that you are connecting your computer to a server which then connects you to the Internet. You can make all the long distance computer connections you want for the cost of making just that first (hopefully local) call! You experience no telephone long distance charges, even when connecting to a computer in Australia, if your ISP is a local call away.

There are, however, limits to the speed of your connection to the Internet using existing telephone technology. A race is on between cable TV companies, satellite and communication services, and even electricity companies to provide Internet access.

Barbara Says:

If one of the faster Internet service technologies is available in your area, check with customers using the service about problems they may have had. Ask questions at computer user groups in your area, and at your local computer store. If the risks of using such leading edge technologies seem worthwhile, then enjoy the speed they can provide.

No matter which technology you use to access the Internet, you will have to learn to use some additional software programs in order to reach everything on the Net. The two most popular programs for browsing the Internet are Netscape Navigator (packaged with most ISP connection/setup software) and Internet Explorer (included with Windows 95/98). Both can be obtained for free. See *Appendix A: Choosing an ISP* starting on page 171 for more information.

Barbara Says:

More and more public libraries, community centers, and even restaurants are offering their patrons (at least partial) Internet access. The high school my daughters attend keeps its library open two nights per week, so parents can learn to surf the Internet, while their children are doing homework. Even if you don't own a computer look around your community for a source of free Internet access.

What does it usually take to get onto the Internet today?

1.   a computer (with a graphical operating system, like Windows or Macintosh)

2.   a modem that lets your computer "talk" to other computers over a regular telephone line (or a special cable box or satellite dish, if you are using an alternate technology)

3.   a telephone jack close to your computer (or an alternate hookup)

4.   communications software (i.e. a Web browser)

5.   an Internet Service Provider (preferably with more than one phone number for access that is a local call for you—if you are using a telephone to call the provider's server computer)

Getting onto the Information Superhighway is the hard part. Once online you'll find cruising the Internet far safer, easier, and more rewarding than cruising the Interstate Highway in your car.

On the World Wide Web, you click a button and surf (browse) from computer to computer around the world. Using simple search engines, you type a keyword or phrase in a box on your screen, then "click" on a button to search around the world. The Internet makes you feel as if Scotty from the Starship Enterprise just beamed you into the future.

Part II: Getting Online

Web Browsers

A Web browser is a software program. Browsers do for the Internet what word processing programs did for typing.

 If you are not a computer expert, stick with standard browser programs like Netscape Navigator or Internet Explorer. Most genealogists would rather not spend time fiddling with their software or on the telephone to technical support. It is especially important to have a name-brand modem, since your biggest challenge will be getting your modem and your ISP's equipment to initially communicate with each other.

Web browsers do exciting things for the Internet explorer. First, they make navigating the "Net" as easy as pointing-and-clicking with a mouse (or other pointing device). Second, they allow you to "jump" from one location to another by clicking on highlighted or underlined words, phrases, or pictures. These are called "hyperlinks" or "links."

 You can tell when your mouse pointer is resting on a link because your pointer turns into a "hand" that looks like this:

What is amazing about browsing the Web is that the page you see could be on any one of the millions of computers around the world connected to the Internet – and you do not need to know which one. Your Web browser and the hyperlinks on the Web pages you visit take care of finding that computer and displaying the pages for you. This is by far the easiest method of navigating the Internet.

Usually either Internet Explorer or Netscape's Web browser is provided free when you sign up with your Internet Service Provider. These browsers are updated periodically and both are available for downloading from the Internet.

Using E-mail Software

E-mail on the Internet works very much like regular postal mail, except it travels electronically. You have an "address" where you receive your e-mail, and you send e-mail to people at their electronic address. You do not need to have your computer on in order to receive e-mail. When someone sends you e-mail, it goes to your Internet Service Provider's server and is stored there until you check for your e-mail.

If you are currently on the Internet, you already have an e-mail address set up for you with your Internet Service Provider (ISP). A typical e-mail address looks something like "**richardw@earthlink.net**." The name before the "@" symbol identifies the recipient of the mail, usually their login ID name. It can be a personal name, nickname, title, or the name of a department or company. The information that follows the "@" symbol identifies the computer (also known as the domain name) to which the e-mail is sent. The extension at the end of the address identifies the type of server to which the e-mail is going. In the United States, these extensions are three letters in length.

Some common U.S. extensions are:

Extension	Server type
.com	Commercial
.edu	Educational
.gov	Government
.net	Network
.org	Nonprofit Organization

Some two-letter geographic extensions used outside the U.S. are:

Extension	Country
.au	Australia
.at	Austria
.ca	Canada
.dk	Denmark
.fi	Finland
.fr	France
.de	Germany
.ie	Ireland
.il	Israel
.it	Italy
.nl	Netherlands
.no	Norway
.se	Sweden
.ch	Switzerland
.uk	United Kingdom

It is helpful for a genealogist to know what these extensions are because it gives them some idea of where their e-mail came from.

If you have used a computer to type a letter, you already have most of the skills you need to send e-mail. The differences appear when you finish typing the message and are ready to send it. With regular mail (snail mail), you must print the letter, put it in an envelope, address it, weigh it, put stamps on it, then put it in a mailbox and wait for a reply.

With e-mail you simply press a key or two and the letter is sent electronically. If the recipient is currently logged onto the Net, he or she can read your letter within a few seconds. It takes less than two hours to send an e-mail message around the world—all for the cost of a local call plus your monthly ISP charge (that you are already paying).

Richard Says:

 I use an e-mail program called Eudora Pro. It is very powerful. I like it because it automatically sorts my e-mail into different mailboxes. It also spell checks my e-mail before I send it. They offer a free version called Eudora Light. Both can be downloaded from their Web site at: **http://www.eudora.com/**.

Barbara Says:

I now use the e-mail program that comes with Internet Explorer called Outlook Express. For years as a graduate student, I used one of the older e-mail programs that worked on our university's computer system. The newer (graphical interface) e-mail programs sure make things easier.

There are many different software programs you can use to send and receive your e-mail. Eudora Pro is one of the top ranked commercial programs for this purpose. There are also many shareware e-mail programs available online. Of course, some e-mail capabilities are included in most Web browser software packages and may meet the average genealogist's needs.

One important consideration is how your software (and service provider) handles e-mail file attachments. If you want to send someone a GEDCOM file, it is nice to be able to attach it to an e-mail message you send. However, not all e-mail software and Internet Service Providers can handle all types of e-mail attachments. Sometimes these attachments are garbled as they pass between Internet Service Providers (because of coding and compression incompatibilities).

If your GEDCOM file arrives as an e-mail attachment and turns out to be unusable, try asking the sender if they can make the GEDCOM file into an executable zip file with PKZip or WinZip and send it again. Our experience is that zipped GEDCOM files transmit cleaner than plain GEDCOM files.

If the GEDCOM file still arrives looking as if a monkey typed it on the keyboard, then we suggest you get the commercial program called E-ttachment Opener (for Windows 95/98 and Windows NT only.) E-ttachment Opener is available at: **http://www.dataviz.com/Products/ETO/ETO_Home.html**. This program beautifully handles both compression and coding problems in e-mail attachments.

When you choose an ISP, you are also choosing your associated e-mail address. Generally your e-mail address is your user login name (the name you use to access your ISP account), followed by the @ symbol, then your ISP's domain name. For example, Richard has an ISP account with EarthLink. He chose the user login name of "richardw." This makes his complete e-mail address **richardw@earthlink.net**, as long as he keeps his account at EarthLink.

Barbara is currently on Microsoft Network (MSN), so her e-mail address is **BarbZR@msn.com**. The MSN server is not case-sensitive. It doesn't care whether people sending her e-mail capitalize her initials or not. Her old e-mail account on the university computer was case-sensitive, so she had to use all lowercase letters in her old e-mail address.

It is a real hassle to change your e-mail address. Perhaps even more of a hassle than changing your snail mail address. If you are on the Internet for a while, you will find yourself signing up for mail lists. You may also register your surnames and e-mail address in online databases. You will post genealogical queries and probably find many other researchers working on your surnames and exchange information with them electronically.

If you then decide to change service providers, your e-mail address will change. Your old e-mail address will cease to exist. It is almost impossible to find everyone who has your old e-mail address to let them know your new e-mail address. So, choose your Internet Service Provider wisely. Make sure you consider what your needs may be in the future. This way you won't rapidly outgrow your ISP.

There are services that give you a permanent e-mail address. Many are free. A few other services let you access your e-mail without having an Internet account. One such service is Hotmail (located at **http://www.hotmail.com/**). They offer you an e-mail address that can be accessed through any Internet Service Provider. So, with Hotmail you get a permanent e-mail address that you can access through any Internet connection and with any Web browser. You can read your e-mail from a local library or at a friend's house over the Internet.

Another free limited e-mail service is available through Juno. They have a Web site with more information (**http://www.juno.com/**). Juno gives you e-mail without access to the Internet. They give you a dial up number you can call from home with your modem to send or receive e-mail. E-mail through Juno cannot have external file attachments. Message size and the volume of daily e-mail are limited.

When faced with an unavoidable change in your e-mail address, consider registering with an Internet directory service (the equivalent of the telephone White Pages). There are many free sites on the Internet where you can register your e-mail address (see the "Locating Living People"section in *Part III,* starting on page 146). Even if you are not changing your e-mail address, this is a good idea. Other genealogists can find you more easily to share information.

A few sites where you can register your e-mail address:

411 Directories: **http://www.four11.com/**

Internet Address Finder: **http://www.iaf.net/**

Switchboard Directory: **http://www.switchboard.com/**

WhoWhere?: **http://www.whowhere.com/**

Mail Lists

Mail lists are discussion groups where the discussions take place via e-mail. Mail lists on the Internet are organized for people to exchange electronic messages about a topic of common interest. Many mail lists are specifically for genealogists.

A Typical Mail List Message (from the Wilson Surname list):

Resent-Date: Fri, 5 Jun 1998 14:20:00 -0700 (PDT)
From: BXGC22B@prodigy.com (MRS ADELENE MULLINS)
Date: Fri, 5 Jun 1998 17:19:05, -0500
Subject: [WILSON-L] Jacob Wilson
To: WILSON-L@rootsweb.com
X-Mailing-List: <WILSON-L@rootsweb.com> archive/latest/1000

Searching for the parents of Jacob Wilson b 1802 in PA, married Rebecca Howell on Jan 15, 1825 in Bracken Co., KY. Could it be James Wilson ? I have a will for a James Wilson who died in Bracken Co., but it does not list the names of the children.

Adelene Mullins

==== WILSON Mailing List ====
7 Ask listowner at sundance@neosoft.com for admin help; please do not have the word digest in the Subject line. Do not replay long posts. Excerpt first two lines or KEY line if referring to prior post. Rural, international subscribers often pay premium -stay ON list topic

---

Large server computers typically host these discussion groups. A list owner moderates many mail lists. Their job is to make sure the messages posted stay on the topic and proper "Netiquette" is observed. See the "Netiquette" section in Part II on page 43 and also in *Part III*, starting on page 67)

If you wanted to subscribe to a mail list such as NORCAL-L (for NORthern CALifornia genealogy discussion list), send the **subscribe** command in the body of an e-mail message to the mail list server that hosts that discussion group. (See the following example).

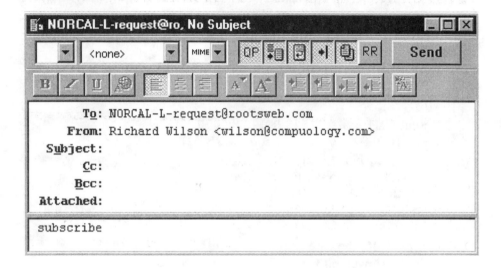

Although you "subscribe" to the mail list, there is no cost involved (other than the time it takes to read the messages). It's like subscribing to a free magazine written by the subscribers.

Therefore, as you can see from the example, to subscribe to a mail list, you simply send an e-mail message to the host computer. Usually all your message needs to say is "subscribe." However with some systems the most you need to type into the body of the message is "subscribe *listname your@address*" (where *listname* is the name of the mail list you want to subscribe to and *your@address* is your e-mail address). See the example that follows.

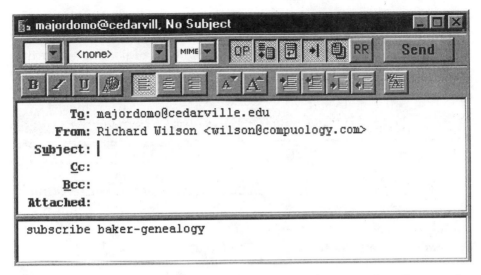

As you can see from the previous example, to subscribe to the BAKER-GENEALOGY mail list for sharing information regarding the BAKER surname (in any place and at any time) you simply send an e-mail message to majordomo@cedarville.edu with the following message: *subscribe baker-genealogy*

An excellent site to check for mail lists and newsgroup topics of genealogical interest can be found at:
http://members.aol.com/johnf14246/gen_mail.html

Mail lists cover topics such as specific surnames, research in specific geographic areas (such as "Virginia Roots" at VA-Roots), or topics of special interest (such as genealogy in general, genealogical computing, research methodology, etc.).

By subscribing to a specific mail list, you are telling the host computer to forward to you all the e-mail messages it receives for that group. Be aware this is usually not the electronic address to which you send a message to be publicly posted. There is usually one electronic address for subscribing, unsubscribing, and changing the settings for your subscription (like digest mode) and a different electronic address you use to post messages to the discussion group for public viewing.

You may receive only a few messages a week, or as many as hundreds per day, depending upon the mail list to which you subscribe. E-mail overload is common among genealogists new to mail lists and the Internet. Subscribe to just a few mail lists at first until you learn to harness the power of your computer by learning to keyword search all the lists of interest to you.

Most ISP's have a limit on the number of messages that your electronic mailbox can hold. If you receive too many messages, your mailbox can get full, causing your e-mail to "bounce." Usually bounced e-mail causes the mail list computer to drop you from that mail list.

When you first subscribe to a mail list, you are sent an e-mail message that includes instructions. Included in these instructions are how to unsubscribe from the mail list, how to post a message to the list, and options available for that list (such as digest mode). Print out these instructions and put them where you can find them. Then you'll have them when you need to unsubscribe from this list. You **will** find yourself needing these instructions eventually.

**Example of a explanatory e-mail message you might get
from the host of a mail list:**

Message-ID: <"Sender"@bl-14.rootsweb.com>
From: WILSON-L@rootsweb.com
X-Mailing-List: <WILSON-L@rootsweb.com> archive/latest/68
Sender: WILSON-L-request@rootsweb.com

WILSON YEAR LOCATION is our format (change it to specifics)
actual year & location per 1st event needs to be replaced in the Subject line as
follows:

WILSON (or a variant SURNAME) is always the FIRST word
the 2nd word may be a first name of the 1st key person described

-or you may go on to just give a key YEAR of 1st person or event described in the
body of the message

Finally, also include a LOCATION for that person/event, for example:

WILLISON, Isaac - born 1690 - Glasgow, SCOTLAND

       ****

THEN you e-mail it to the ADDRESS:

WILSON-L@rootsweb.com

with details in the body of the message per the family history connected to the topic
of this list in terms of what the Subject is - you may include details of that person,
their family, connections and collaterals, spouses, children, ancestors, events, name
spellings and origins, stories of places with family name, census data, wills, deed,
births, marriages, deaths and obituaries, places lived, occupations, education,
personalities, biographies on topic, books, reunions, genetics (e.g. twins, etc.)
military service, travels, migrations, adoptions, neighbors, churches, cemeteries, or
other items the listowner approves per guideline. Stay on topic. Do not send
attachments. We will help-just ask if you need clarification - please share data,
queries and credit sources.

If you list any URL please excerpt ON TOPIC details explicitly connected in
your excerpt here per the focus of this list. Do not post solicitations for other off
topic lists items or lost people -ask the listowner privately if you lose mail or have
admin problems. If a prior poster did not follow these directions, send them a copy
& CHANGE your Subject line so the FIRST word begins with a SURNAME.

Types of genealogical mail lists:
- Surname
- Country
- State/Province
- County
- Ethnic/Special interest
- Genealogical computing

Again, remember the address to which you send an e-mail message for posting on a mail list is usually **not** the same address you send a message to when you are subscribing or unsubscribing from that list.

Some mail lists can send you the messages they receive in a consolidated format called "digest" mode. In digest mode, you get only one or two groups of messages forwarded per day (depending on how active the mail list is).

When a mail list forwards its messages to you in digest mode, it often starts with the subject lines (short descriptions of each message) from all the included messages. Then it lists the actual messages. However, some mail lists in digest mode just send you the actual messages listed in one big e-mail message per day.

On the next page, we have included an example of a digest mode mail list message with an index of subject lines. The advantage of having an index of subject lines (message headers) is that you can quickly see if you have an interest in reading any of the included messages.

Example of Digest mode messages:

Date: Mon, 10 Mar 1997 00:03:24 -0500
Sender: Genealogy Computing Discussion List
<GENCMP-L@MAIL.EWORLD.COM>
From: Automatic digest processor <LISTSERV@MAIL.EWORLD.COM>
Subject: GENCMP-L Digest - 8 Mar 1997 to 9 Mar 1997
To: Recipients of GENCMP-L digests
<GENCMP-L@MAIL.EWORLD.COM>

There are 11 messages totaling 289 lines in this issue.

Topics of the day:

  1. Family Gathering 1.1 Update
  2. EMAIL DOMAIN NAME
  3. Please suggest a program to use with Cyrillic alphabet
  4. GENCMP-L Digest - 8 Mar 1997
  5. Netiquette

[in digest mode the above 5 messages would follow this summary]

**[First the subjects of all the messages are listed for the current digest.
Then the actual messages follow.]**

Remember, anything you post to a mail list can and will be read around the world. Your punctuation and speelng <grin> will be visible to all. Observe proper Netiquette. Send private messages directly to the person with whom you wish to communicate. Only post messages of general interest to the mail list.

Mail lists can be very useful, but you have to be careful that you do not get so much e-mail that you cannot possibly read it all—even if it is predigested <grin>. It is very easy to get more e-mail than you could ever read when you sign up for multiple genealogical mail lists.

Time is a four-letter word for most genealogists. Reading mail lists takes time. However, if you use any of the major word processing programs, you have a tool that can save you time and eyestrain.

 Let your e-mail digests pile up for a week. Highlight all of them in your e-mail program and save them as one big text file. Import this text file into your word processor.

In **WORD 97**, go to EDIT then FIND in the pull down menu. In the box that appears, you have several options: find words that match the case of the word (or SURNAME) you enter; find whole words only (so the surname HOUGH is not found as part of "though"); find words that sound like the word you enter; or find all word forms that match. Thus, you can search the whole text file for any keyword you specify in your word processor.

In **WordPerfect 8**, go to EDIT then FIND AND REPLACE in the pull down menu. This opens a box where you type the word that you want to find. You can also pull down the MATCH menu and select CASE if you want to match the case of the word (or SURNAME) you have entered.

It can and does pay dividends to use mail lists on the Internet. Genealogists exchange questions and queries about that mail list's topic. This is also a place for sharing original research and years of experience.

Messages from many genealogical mail lists are archived (saved) on the Rootsweb server. To search the archive of these saved messages go to: **http://www.rootsweb.com/rootsweb/searches/**. You will want to check out this site because it also allows you to perform searches on many other databases and archives at Rootsweb.

Consider purchasing e-mail indexing software such as Whew!. This program only costs $9.95. Download it off the Internet from the **http://www.wordcruncher.com/** Web site. It works with most current versions of major e-mail software programs (Eudora Pro 3 or 4, Exchange, Netscape Mail 3 or 4, Outlook, and Outlook Express). Whew! creates an every word index of all the e-mail stored by these programs on your computer. It then allows you to do advanced searches using that index, including proximity searches (something current word processor programs can't do). You can even copy and paste your keyword list into Whew! to do multiple searches.

Barbara Says:

If you have a keyword list that you have refined over the years, you already have something to start from as you electronically search mail lists and newsgroup messages. My keyword lists include not only the surnames (and their spelling variations) that I am researching, but also the county names and subject words (like "iron" and "forge") that describe occupations.

This method is not perfect. You will miss a few messages that would be of interest to you. Nevertheless it makes up in quantity what it lacks in quality. By using the "match case" feature for the surname DICK, I avoid having to look at the nickname Dick that appears all too often in messages on mail lists. I'm lucky that my ancestors Adonijah THOMAS, Micajah WILSON, and Patience Lowery SMITH have unusual given names to go with their common surnames. I search for occurrences of their given names in the messages rather than looking at all the entries for THOMASes, WILSONs and SMITHs.

I keep different keyword lists to search Roots-L, VA-Roots, and TN-Roots. Roots-L is the granddaddy of all genealogy mail lists. It is a general genealogy discussion list. It pays to read the Roots-L digest summaries.

It takes about thirty minutes per week to search these three mail lists. In the past year, I have electronically met some generous cousins who have shared research and added three new surnames to the pedigree that I have worked on for twenty-seven years.

Genealogists who use mail lists on the Internet will reap rewards but only after sifting through much sand and gravel to get to the nuggets of gold.

Newsgroups

One of the first e-mail areas created on the Internet was Usenet. Usenet is a collection of electronic discussion groups called "newsgroups." (The terms Usenet and newsgroup are used interchangeably.) It is one of the busiest areas on the Internet with more than 32,000 separate newsgroups, each covering a different topic.

Partial list of genealogy newsgroups:

alt.war.civil.usa
alt.adoption (for adoptees, birthparents, adoptive parents)
alt.genealogy (general genealogy topics).
alt.scottish.clans
fido.eur.genealogy
fido.ger.genealogy
fr.rec.genealogie (French-speaking people, mostly in French).
rec.heraldry
sfnet.harrastus.sukututkimus (mostly in Finnish)
soc.genealogy.african
soc.genealogy.britain
soc.genealogy.computing (genealogical computing and Net resources).
soc.genealogy.german
soc.genealogy.hispanic
soc.genealogy.ireland
soc.genealogy.italian
soc.genealogy.jewish
soc.genealogy.marketplace
soc.genealogy.methods (genealogy methods and non-net resources)
soc.genealogy.misc (general genealogical discussions that don't fit within
                one of the other soc.genealogy.* newsgroups).

Usually a newsgroup's name tells you something about the content of its discussions. Major categories for newsgroup discussion topics are: *comp* (computer), *rec* (recreation), *soc* (sociality) or *biz* (business). Most of the genealogy topics are in the *soc.genealogy* section of online newsgroups.

Some of the topics available in genealogical newsgroups include genealogical computing, surnames, geographic areas, and genealogy methods.

Newsgroups, like mail lists, use e-mail messages sent to a host computer. Unlike mail lists, however, newsgroups do not forward the messages to your e-mail address. Unless you have special software, you must logon to the computer hosting that newsgroup and download (retrieve to your computer) the headers (subject lines) of the e-mail messages recently posted. The subject line of each message should indicate what that message is about. Reading the headers allows you to select only those messages you are interested in reading. Once you decide which messages you want to read, you must be online (or go back online) to retrieve those messages, one at a time, to read them.

When you send an e-mail message to a newsgroup or mail list the header (subject line) is the most important part of your message. Keep the header short. In addition, when sending questions about research subjects, be sure to include a **name,** a **date,** and a **place** in the header.

To place a message on the newsgroup for public viewing you send an e-mail message addressed to that group at the host computer and it will be "posted" for everyone to read. People can reply to your message in one of two ways. Either they can send you a private e-mail message at your personal e-mail address, or they can send an e-mail message to the newsgroup for everyone to see and read, just like on a mail list.

Typical message posted to a newsgroup (from alt.genealogy):

Have found about a dozen family photographs relating to a HUGHES family that lived in Reading, PA circa 1870-1920. Is anyone researching HUGHES in this location? I would like to reunite these photos with a researcher. Here are some of the first names: Ann Valentine, Alice M., Emily, L. G., Louis McK., F.D. Hughes, Nettie V. Any help to locate family information which would help locate descendants is appreciated.
Carol <getback@telusplanet.net>

Your e-mail message and the replies it receives form "threads" of conversations.The next example shows a newsgroup listing from the **soc.genealogy.computing** newsgroup.

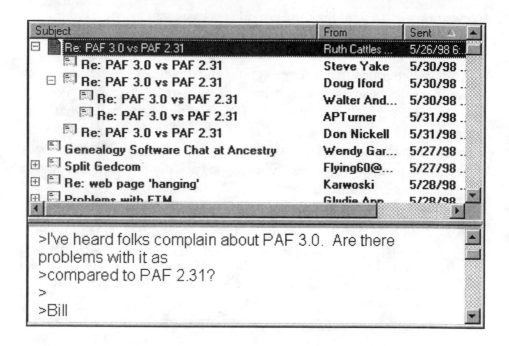

Subject	From	Sent
Re: PAF 3.0 vs PAF 2.31	Ruth Cattles ...	5/26/98 6:
Re: PAF 3.0 vs PAF 2.31	Steve Yake	5/30/98 .
Re: PAF 3.0 vs PAF 2.31	Doug Iford	5/30/98 .
Re: PAF 3.0 vs PAF 2.31	Walter And...	5/30/98 .
Re: PAF 3.0 vs PAF 2.31	APTurner	5/31/98 .
Re: PAF 3.0 vs PAF 2.31	Don Nickell	5/31/98 .
Genealogy Software Chat at Ancestry	Wendy Gar...	5/27/98 .
Split Gedcom	Flying60@...	5/27/98 .
Re: web page 'hanging'	Karwoski	5/28/98 .
Problems with FTM	Gludie Ann	5/28/98

>I've heard folks complain about PAF 3.0. Are there problems with it as
>compared to PAF 2.31?
>
>Bill

In this example, the original message (highlighted) has three replies (shown inset one level to the right) then one of those replies has two replies to it (inset one more level). These threads form running discussions maintained on the newsgroup for a period of time. There are special software programs available to make reading these "threaded" newsgroup conversations easier. This type of software makes message threads easy to follow by displaying them in a hierarchical (indented) format and/or in different colors.

Both Netscape Navigator and Internet Explorer have built-in newsgroup reading capabilities. But they are not as powerful as software programs written specifically for this purpose.

When you first run your newsreader program it should ask if you want to download the new newsgroups that are available, select "Yes" (otherwise, you will only have a few default newsgroups to look at). Be aware that it will take a while to download because there are over 30,000 groups. To download the groups do the following:

Internet Explorer 4 (Outlook Express):
Select Newsgroups . . . from the Tools pull-down menu.
The "Newsgroups" box will appear.
With the "All" tab selected, press the "Reset List" button.

Netscape Communicator 4 (Collabra Discussion Groups):
Select Subscribe to Discussion Groups . . . from the File pull-down menu.
The "Subscribe to Discussion Groups" box will appear.
With the "All Groups" tab selected, press the "Reset List" button.

Be aware that if you do not read the newsgroup postings for a few weeks, you may miss replies to your messages. Messages are periodically removed from the list as they get older. Newsgroups, unlike mail lists, often are not archived for later searching.

You can get to newsgroups from Netscape Navigator by selecting "Netscape News" from the "Window" pull-down menu. From Internet Explorer you access newsgroups by selecting "Read News" from the "Go" pull-down menu. You can usually access newsgroups from your browser's URL window by typing in the word "**news:**" and then the name of the newsgroup you want to read (i.e., **news:soc.genealogy.surnames**).

Barbara Says:

> There is a software program called NewsRover (that is available on the Internet at **http://www.NewsRover.com/**) that automates your searches in newsgroups. NewsRover allows genealogists to create custom keyword lists and specify which newsgroups to search in for those keywords. This software program downloads only messages with your keywords from the specified newsgroup(s) This allows you to view them at a time convenient to you. NewsRover even highlights your keywords in the messages downloaded. NewsRover is well worth the $29.95 I paid for it because of the time and eyestrain it saves me.

Richard Says:

> The popular Web browsers don't have enough special features to make using newsgroups easy; therefore, I recommend the use of a separate newsgroup software program for reading newsgroups. The newsgroup reader I use is called *Free Agent*. There is no cost to download and use it. *Free Agent* has many good features. You can download it at: **http://www.forteinc.com/getfa/download.htm**

Newsgroups and mail lists are tremendous resources for getting specific answers to questions about virtually any subject. Just post a question and one or more people will answer it. We have found genealogists extremely generous with their help. Remember, however, that the advice givers will have varying degrees of expertise and experience.

If it sounds as if mail lists and newsgroups are a lot alike, that is because they are. Both consist of e-mail messages about a specified topic sent to a host computer via the Internet. The main difference between newsgroups and mail lists is how you receive the messages. Mail lists automatically send their messages to your e-mail address for you to read whenever you wish. Newsgroup messages require you to go to the newsgroup and read them while online. Some genealogical topics are only available as mail lists, and others are only available as newsgroups.

Another difference between mail lists and newsgroups is that there are far fewer newsgroups that are specifically for genealogy. There are over 32,000 newsgroups, but only a few dozen newsgroups about genealogical topics. There are thousands of mail lists specifically for genealogical topics.

 There are many places on the Internet to place free queries. Mail lists, newsgroups, and the county pages in the USGenWeb Project all allow you to post free queries. Because of the volume of queries found in these areas, be sure to include a name, a date, and a place (where your ancestor lived) in every query you post. Otherwise, your query will be ignored by busy genealogists.

Chat Sessions

Chat sessions operate a little like e-mail, you use your computer to type electronic messages to other users. The major difference is that with chat sessions everyone sending and receiving messages must be online and connected to the session at the same time.

To be able to participate in a Chat, you usually need to download and install a freeware or shareware program, such as the Ichat program (available from **http://www.ichat.com/**). This program works in conjunction with your Web browser software and allows you to participate in live, online conversations via the typed word.

Chat sessions for genealogical topics are becoming more popular. In the past, you could have a genealogy chat on AOL or other commercial providers, but you were limited to only those people with access to their system. Today more and more chat sessions are open to all genealogists.

The advantages to chat are that you can get immediate answers to your questions without having to wait for someone to return your e-mail message. However, there are a few limitations with chat. You are limited to answers from only those who happen to be online at the same time you ask the question. If too many people ask questions (before the answer to a previous question is given) it becomes very confusing. Chat sessions can get a bit "noisy" with conversations crossing over each other.

Netiquette

Mail lists, newsgroups, and chat sessions are public forums. They have social mores. Netiquette is the recommended etiquette for genealogists who participate on the Internet. Remember the messages you send to any of these discussion groups are posted for anyone to view, anywhere in the world.

Barbara Says:

To avoid public embarrassment, read the posted messages for a week or more before sending in your own messages. Otherwise, you **will** be flamed if you inadvertently commit a faux pas!

One of the first rules of Netiquette is that typing in all capital letters is the equivalent of SHOUTING on the Internet. Many genealogy discussion groups (but not all) make an exception in the case of SURNAMES, which usually **should** be typed in capital letters.

Barbara Says:

Please follow this convention of typing only SURNAMES in caps, when allowed. That way genealogists will find only the surname DICK and not the nickname for Richard when they do keyword searches.

FTP - What is it? Do I have it?

FTP does for the genealogist what a good Chesapeake Bay Retriever does for a duck hunter. It goes out into the cold cruel waters of various computer interfaces on the Internet and retrieves what you send it out to get. FTP makes many types of files and free software readily available to genealogists at the push of a button. It also makes possible live chat areas on the Internet.

FTP stands for File Transfer Protocol. FTP is a program, as well as a set of procedures or rules, for transferring files between computers over the Internet. Specifically, it is the set of rules that govern how files are copied from one computer to another.

When given the choice of using FTP or HTTP to download a file, choose FTP because it is usually faster.

Richard Says:

In some cases, you may want to use a separate FTP program to copy files. Stand-alone FTP programs have capabilities that are beyond the limited FTP features built into the Web browsers we have today. You will also need additional software to participate in chat areas on the Internet, such as those found at **http://www.ancestry.com** for genealogists.

Web browsers have some FTP capabilities built-in. Whenever you click on any link (be it a link to a text, program, or graphics file), a copy of that file is automatically transferred to your computer. That is how your computer is able to "read" Web pages. Your computer temporarily downloads these files and brings them up on your screen.

Richard Says:

Keep in mind that Web browsers store such files only temporarily. If you want to save a file permanently, go to "File" and choose "Save As . . ." Once you give it a name and location, the file is saved on your computer.

Barbara Says:

Lucky us today. Be glad you didn't have to transfer files over the Internet in the old days before Web browsers! Today transferring files takes just a point and a click (and sometimes a VISA card number. <grin>)

Use FTP to download graphics off the Internet. When you see a graphic you want to capture to your computer, point to it with your mouse. Click the right mouse button and select "Save As . . ." Give the graphic file a name and a location for storage, and it will then be saved on your hard drive.

 Copyright Warning:

Be aware that many files and graphics on the Internet are copyrighted. Make sure what you are downloading does not violate any copyright laws. More information on copyrights is at: **http://lcweb.loc.gov/copyright/**
(See also the "Copyright Information" sites in *Part III* of this book on page 143).

Another reason genealogists need to know how to use FTP is to publish their genealogies on the World Wide Web. Once you have designed your Web pages, you then use an FTP program to upload (send) the files (Web pages) you have created to the Internet server (host computer) where you are renting space. Once your Web page files are set up (stored) on the server, they become readable by anyone with World Wide Web access (even Macintosh users)!

Richard Says:

I like the full-featured FTP program called WS_FTP. It is available in both Windows 3.x and Windows 95/98 versions. It is shareware and available for downloading on the Internet for free home use at:
http://www.ipswitch.com/downloads.html#WS_FTP

There are two types of FTP used on the Internet today. They are Anonymous FTP (see page 177 for the definition of Anonymous FTP) and regular FTP. Anonymous FTP makes it possible to copy actual (digitized) Bible records from the Library of Virginia. You will need a viewer (yes, yet another piece of software) to be able to read this type of graphic file. You can't just read it with your word processor. Most word processors can handle only a limited number of different graphic file formats.

 In order to access the Internet with **regular FTP**, you must have the address of the computer where the FTP files are stored, a user name and a password to logon to that computer. If you use Netscape as your FTP program, you would put the user name and password in the configuration for FTP. To do this, select the "Options" pull-down menu. Select "Editor Preferences" then the "Publish" tab (in Editor Preferences). You then put in the FTP address, user name and password.

There are hundreds of thousands of files (many of interest to genealogists) stored and made available for researchers to freely download from Anonymous FTP sites on computers around the world. One example of such an Anonymous FTP site is located on the SpryNet/CompuServe FTP Server at **ftp://ftp.spry.com/pub/**. This is a useful site for genealogists to obtain software for DOS, Windows 3.x, Windows 95/98, and Macintosh computers.

Anonymous FTP sites can be used to find and copy software, documents, graphics, and many types of information from the Internet to your home computer. Keep in mind universities and other research sites spent years generating files in the old Telnet days. Some of these files are of particular interest to genealogists. Moreover, they can be accessed more easily today than ever before via your Web browser's FTP capabilities.

If you are new to the FTP concept, you may want to run through this exercise to practice viewing a file with anonymous FTP:

- Select the FTP site for the Library of Congress. To do this you type the URL which is **ftp://ftp.loc.gov/** into the appropriate box on your browser and press <ENTER>.

- This then connects you to the Library of Congress FTP site. You will see a typical computer directory listing the files and subdirectories accessible from that point.

- Scroll down the list to the "pub/" subdirectory and click on it.

- Once in the "pub/" directory, scroll down to the subdirectory titled "reference.guides/" and click on it.

- Having arrived at the "reference.guides/" directory, click on "stars.and.stripes." This text file about the holdings of the *Stars and Stripes* newspaper will then be displayed on your computer screen via FTP. If you want to keep this file, you must give it a name and store it on your hard drive.

Surfing vs. Searching the Internet

The Internet wasn't very old before it grew to be so large that some method for finding information (stored on computers linked to the Internet) was needed. To meet this need, several different tools evolved such as Gopher, Veronica, and Archie. These tools were essential for searching the Internet in pre-Web days. They have largely been superceded by the more full-featured Internet search tools of today (see "Internet Search Tools" in *Part III* starting on page 152).

There are three basic ways to navigate the World Wide Web:

- Type a URL you have found in the space provided in your Web browser and press <ENTER>

- Use hyperlinks to surf (browse) from site to site on the Web

- Use a search engine to find sites containing the keywords for which you are searching

There are two basic ways to find the URLs of Web sites:

- Word of mouth

- Printed in publications

Genealogists love getting together with other genealogists wherever they may meet (at meetings of local societies and special interest groups, in seminars and conferences, or online in chat areas). They are quick to share tips on hot Web sites that they have found.

Expand your horizons. Watch for helpful URLs not only in traditional genealogical publications, but also in newer types of publications brought about by the Internet revolution.

Types of printed publications that often list URLs for Web sites:

- General publications (like *The Genealogical Helper*)
- Geographic publications (like *Tennessee Ancestors*)
- Genealogical computing publications (like *COMPU.GEN*)
- Surname publications (like *Sharp Points*)
- Special interest publications (like *The Record* by NARA)
- Computer/Internet magazines (like *Internet World*)

Don't forget publications that come to you via e-mail:

- Electronic newsletters (like *Eastman's Online Genealogy Newsletter*)
- Mail lists (like the large *Roots-L* discussion group)
- Newsgroups (like *soc.genealogy.computing*)

An good source for genealogical sites is What's Really New in WWW Genealogy Pages (**http://www.genhomepage.com/really_new.html**). (See "Genealogy Megasites" in *Part III* starting on page 68).

Today hyperlinks make surfing the World Wide Web easy. These links make information stored on computers around the world just a point and a click away. With a few educated guesses and a bit of experience, such Internet "surfing" can become productive browsing, especially when you start from genealogy megasites on the Internet.

Genealogy megasites make surfing to sites of interest to genealogists easy. Three excellent genealogy megasites to start from are:

- All-in-One Genealogy Search Page
http://www.geocities.com/Heartland/Acres/8310/gensearcher.html

GenSearcher's All-in-One Genealogy Search Page provides links to some of the best searchable genealogy databases on the Internet.

- USGenWeb or World GenWeb Project
   http://www.usgenweb.org/
   http://www.worldgenweb.org/

These projects gather together links to country, state, and county level genealogy Web sites. This is an all-volunteer organization. These Web sites provide free queries and links to some of the best research helps. State USGenWeb pages typically provide links to that state's archives and/or state library. County USGenWeb sites provide information about and/or links to local genealogical and historical societies. The USGenWeb and World GenWeb projects maintain online archives of searchable files, including census, cemetery, military, land, probate, and obituary records among others.

- Cyndi's List of Genealogy Sites on the Internet
  http://www.cyndislist.com/

Cyndi's List by Cyndi Howell has more than 29,350 links in more than ninety categories. (May she live long and prosper for all the hours per day she puts in keeping this free Web site going!)

 Most of the Web sites mentioned in this book are free. We'll be sure to tell you when we list one that charges a fee.

Internet directories, such as Yahoo! (**http://www.yahoo.com/**) and Cyndi's List, help genealogists be more effective in their browsing. Internet directories are made by humans who review Web sites and catalog them in a hierarchy of subjects. When you do a search on Yahoo!, it looks in its directory for categories that contain your keyword, for sites that contain your keyword in their titles, and lastly for sites that have your keyword in their descriptions. Yahoo!'s categories can help you get ideas for more specific searches if you are exploring a new genealogical subject that you don't know much about.

The disadvantage to surfing or browsing on the Internet for genealogical information is that it takes time and patience to achieve success. It is difficult to tell about the contents of a Web site from its title. Often Web site descriptions do not go into sufficient detail to benefit genealogists making surname specific or location specific searches. These factors place limitations on the usefulness of Internet directories, such as Yahoo!, for genealogists.

Setting Bookmarks using
Internet Explorer or Netscape Communicator:

Internet Explorer 4: When you have located the Web page you want to set a book mark for:

Select "<u>A</u>dd to Favorites . . . " from the "F<u>a</u>vorites" pull-down menu (The "Add Favorite" box will appear).
Select the "Ok" button and the Web page will be book marked.

Netscape Communicator 4: When you have located a Web page you want to set a book mark for:

Select the "Bookmarks" button from the tool bar (at the top left). Select "Add Bookmark" from the list and the Web page will be book marked.

Barbara Says:

Sometimes you have to go to a related site before you start searching for specific information on uncommon topics or surnames. For example, you would have to go to the FEEFHS (Federation of East European Family History Societies) site and use their own site specific index to find anything on the ZUCKNICKs who lived near what is today Cycow, Lublin, Poland. You can find them at **http://www.feefhs.org/** .

Genealogists often find that the Internet contains an overabundance of riches for them. Searching the Net can be an intimidating and frustrating experience. (But not as frustrating as initially getting your computer and modem connected to your ISP). There seems to be a Murphy's Law for Internet searches. They turn up either hundreds of thousands of possible matches or none at all (when you know there must be something somewhere out there about your subject or name).

If you find a Web site that you think might be useful in the future, take the time to bookmark it. Bookmarking a Web site with your browser software means that you can find it again later. As your number of bookmarks grows, organize them into folders by subject using your browser software. This takes time and a little bit of work, but failing to do so means frustration later when you can't find that site without a prodigious amount of time and effort spent looking for it again.

The other major method for finding information on the Internet is keyword searching with search engines. Yahoo! is not a search engine. By definition, search engines are created by machines. Computer programs called worms, robots, crawlers, and spiders (yuck!) are sent out to relentlessly comb the WWW. They crawl twenty-four hours per day through any Web sites they find and index them. Some of these programs index just the main (home) Web page. Others index the entire Web site.

Lycos (**http://www.lycos.com/**), one of the earliest search engines, was created in May 1994. Alta Vista (**http://www.altavista.digital.com/**), another powerful search engine, began in late 1995. Although search engines are a relatively new phenomena (as is the World Wide Web), many have managed to catalog millions of Web pages with their indexing programs. This makes them very useful.

A typical search engine contains:

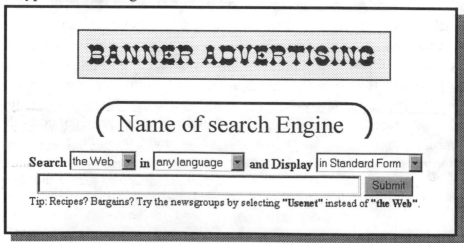

Almost all search engines allow you to begin with a simple search. You type keywords in a box and click on a "search" button to start searching. Most search engines currently available on the Internet can be used free of charge. It is rare to come across a search engine that charges for their searches. If so, it will ask for your credit card number and allow you to exit gracefully if you are not interested in paying for the search.

There are three different strategies for using search engines. One strategy is to go to the larger search engines (such as HotBot or Alta Vista) which claim to have indexed a major portion of the WWW and hope the sheer volume of matches will lead you to something useful.

The second strategy is to use one of the faster search engines and refine your search with that search engine's advanced search features (newer search engines tend to be less busy and therefore faster). Advanced search features include case sensitivity, phrases, adjacencies, proximity, Boolean operators, required terms, prohibited terms, wildcards, and ranking. Not all (or even most) search engines offer all these advanced search features.

A third strategy is to use one of the new meta search engines. A meta search engine allows you to type your search terms just once. It configures that search for use with many different search engines then searches them simultaneously for you. You get dozens of searches for just the effort of making one query.

Each search engine is different with regard to the sites it finds, how much of each Web page it indexes, and the refinements it uses for keyword searches. This means that no one search engine is best for every type of genealogical search on the Internet.

 One way to quickly determine if a search engine is determining matches based upon the site having EVERY word you input or ANY word you input is to set the search for **pizza genealogy** and count the number of hits (matches) the search engine comes up with. If it finds many matches for these two disparate terms, you know it's using ANY term you input for the search.

Some of the common refinements in keyword searches include:

Case sensitivity: This helps you distinguish between the surname HILL and the place name Cherry Hill, NJ. The Alta Vista search engine does case-sensitive searches.

Phrases: Placing double quote marks around a phrase such as "George Washington" typically will find only occurrences of both words in that order. This option will **not** include matches of every site that mentions the word "George" plus every site that mentions the name "Washington," as in the Washington Monument. It would **not** find "Washington George." Most search engines allow you to search on phrases, rather than just individual words. This is handy, since more search engines seem to be set to default to an "OR" setting, rather than an "AND" setting. An "OR" setting means a match if the site includes any of the query terms. An "AND" setting means both terms must be present for that Web site to be considered a match.

Adjacency: This means the query terms must be immediately adjacent to each other. The difference between this option and the "Phrase" option is that with adjacency the terms may be in any order. Example: adjacency will find *Knox County* and *County of Knox* (usually ignoring punctuation and common words like "of").

Proximity: Different search engines use different degrees of proximity. Some search engines set their searches so that the specified terms must be within one hundred words of each other. Other search engines allow you to set the proximity with a **NEAR/n** command, with **n** being the number of words away permissible for the second query term. Example: when searching for Patience Lowry SMITH who was married in Blount County, TN in 1825, you might search for SMITH NEAR/10 Blount.

Boolean operators: Many search engines were originally set up to allow you to use the classic **AND, OR, NOT**, and **NEAR** statements from Boolean algebra. The tendency now is for Internet search engines to provide for the selection of such advanced search features in a box menu. This is a lot easier than setting up a workable algebraic equation with the proper syntax. <grin>

Required terms: A "required term" symbol tells the search engine that the term, which immediately follows the designated symbol, **must** be in the document. Example: SMITH +Blount for any mention of SMITHs in Blount Co., TN. No space is left between the + sign and the required term that follows it.

Prohibited terms: A "prohibited term" symbol tells the search engine that the term that immediately follows the designated symbol must **not** be on the page. Example: MALLARD –duck. Again, no space is left between the – sign and the prohibited term that follows it.

Wildcards: Alta Vista uses the * symbol as a wildcard which replaces up to five additional letters in a word. For example, searching for LINDS* on the Alta Vista search engine would find LINDSAY and LINDSEY, but also LINDSTROM. Other search engines use different keyboard symbols and rules for their wildcard searches.

Rankings: Many search engines use a mathematical formula to guess at the probable relevance of each match found. These formulas are based on such criteria as: whether the query terms were found within the first few words in a site, whether one or more of the search terms are in close proximity to each other at that site, or on the basis of the total number of times your query terms appear in that site.

Each search engine has specific rules for its keyword searches. Unfortunately, most of the current search engines use different rules. These differences make it difficult to learn to use many search engines. A winning strategy is to pick one of the top search engines and learn to use it well. When that search engine doesn't work for you (or is busy and you can't get on to do a search), try one of the other search engines.

Three good search engines for genealogical searches are HotBot (**http://www.hotbot.com/**), Excite (**http://www.excite.com/**), and Alta Vista (**http://altavista.digital.com/**).

Search Engine Features Table			
	Alta Vista	Excite	HotBot
Default	OR (any)	OR (any)	via menu
Inclusion	+ or AND	+	via menu
Exclusion	- or AND NOT	via menu	via menu
Phrase	"quote marks"	via menu	via menu
Proximity	NEAR (within 10)	(not available)	(not available)
Wild Cards	*	(not available)	(not available)
Other Features	case sensitivity	concept searches	easy to use

All too often, search engines seem to hide their help files. They also seem to hide the buttons to click on for advanced search settings behind images of spiders, bugs, or seemingly non-related graphics. Simply move your cursor over the page, watching for it to change into the shape of a pointing hand. This indicates there are links to help files, advanced search features, or the next page of possible matches. Your teenagers, who are used to playing video games, may be able to help you if you get stuck and can't figure out what to do next.

Many search engines give you a choice to search the WWW, Usenet newsgroups, archived files and databases, or all of the above. Most search engines allow you to start with simple searches and then refine your search with the advanced search features described above.

Some search engines (such as Excite) claim to allow you to search by concept and not just keywords. Other search engines (such as Webcrawler) claim you can do "natural language searching." They use a thesaurus of concepts, which can be very helpful. Still others (like Lycos) don't employ sophisticated searches at all, but rely on the size of their indexes for success. They are quite often effective in finding what you are searching for because of their sheer size.

Some search engines achieve popularity because they are faster or seem easier to use. Others achieve popularity with their size or advanced search features. No one search engine does it all.

The All-in-One Search Page created by William D. Cross and located at **http://www.albany.net/allinone/** standardizes the advanced search features of several different search engines. It allows you to search 120 of the Internet's best engines, databases, and indexes from a single site.

Quarterdeck's WebCompass software does the same, but costs $49.95 (**http://arachnid.qdeck.com/qdeck/products/wc20/**). Simply enter your query terms and WebCompass sends off your search to multiple search engines and compiles their most probable matches for you.

Barbara Says:

Genealogists will appreciate the new All-In-One Genealogy Search Page that copies this new trend. It is located at:
http://www.geocities.com/Heartland/Acres/8310/gensearcher.html

Most genealogists find themselves using a combination of these three Internet search techniques: finding and typing URLs, surfing (or educated browsing), and searching. Increasingly, the Internet makes it possible for genealogists to pursue their family trees from the convenience of their homes.

A few final words about using search engines:

- Commonly used words make poor query terms for searches. Don't try searching on the word "Web." You will have more success if you narrow your search with a search engine's advanced search features.

- Study the search features of two or three search engines and learn to use at least one really well. When a keyword or phrase works poorly on one search engine, you will be ready to try it on another search engine with different search features.

- Some search engines specialize in a geographic region (like EuroSeek at **http://www.euroseek.net/** for Europe). Other search engines (like

Alta Vista and Excite) offer the option on their home page to search in another language. You may find sites in this way to help you trace your ancestry in that region of the world.

- The Web itself contains a wealth of information on how to use search engines to make your searches better. Use the Web to learn about techniques for searching the Web.

Here are some sites to help you learn more about using search engines:

Using Search Engines on the Internet located at:
   http://www.acld.lib.fl.us/afnhelp/help/search.html

University of Arizona Library help using search engines at:
   http://dizzy.library.arizona.edu/library/guides/engines.htm

How to Search the Web: A Guide to Search Tools at:
   http://issfw.palomar.edu/Library/TGSEARCH.HTM

The Spiders' Apprentice: How to Use Web Search Engines at:
   http://www.monash.com/spidap3.html

When your search finds too FEW matches:

- Make sure you spelled your query terms correctly.

- Make your search less specific (or possibly more specific) with synonyms or spelling variations for names.

- Go back and reread the description of the rules and restrictions of that search engine's features then apply some of those advanced search features.

- If the above modifications still don't produce results, try using a different search engine.

When your search finds too MANY matches:

- Select different keywords that narrow your subject.

- Eliminate common words.

- Use more keywords in your search.

- Use advanced search features to restrict your search.

Search engines, megasites, and directories make exploring new territory on the Internet simple. What are you waiting for? Simply type in your query terms and then click on the **"Search"** button and a world of resources will come to you.

Part III: Internet Resources for Genealogists

Internet Resources

This is not meant to be an all-encompassing list of every site of genealogical interest on the Web. Our purpose is to include enough examples to give you an idea of the possibilities that exist in each category. If you have any additional categories to add to this list, please feel free to contact the authors at **wilson@compuology.com**.

Due to the constantly changing nature of the Internet, there is no guarantee that all of these links will work. At the time of publication, every link was checked and verified to be correct. Check the Web site at **http://www.compuology.com/otherweb.htm** for the most recent URLs.

If you are having trouble loading a Web site, check the spelling, punctuation, and case carefully. If someone gives you the address of **www.latimes.com**, you would have to enter **http://www.latimes.com**. Many people don't mention the **http://** because they assume it is common knowledge that Web sites usually start with **http://**.

Netscape allows you to type in just the name of the site. In the above example, you could just type in the word "latimes" and press enter. Netscape would then find the site: **http://www.latimes.com/**

If someone gives you the address **http://www.times.com.index.html**, you should know that after the site extension (.com) there should be a / (forward slash) and not a . (period). So you should type **http://www.times.com/index.html** to get to that site. (See the table on page 22 for common Internet extension names.)

BIG TIP: You do not have to type all of these dreadful looking electronic addresses. You can go to "Richard Wilson's Other Genealogy Web Sites" page on the Internet. It is located at: **http://www.compuology.com/otherweb.htm** and you will find most of the links in this book. Simply click on the links and go to these Web pages. These links will be updated as we find changes in the URLs for these sites.

General Genealogy Sites

Ancestors Found!:
http://members.tripod.com/~ancestors_found/index.html

Ancestors Found! is a Web site set up to be a lost and found for family photos, Bibles and items of genealogical interest, such as birth certificates or DAR Membership plaques.

Calendar of Genealogical Events:
http://genealogy.emcee.com/PAF/www/events

This genealogy calendar describes upcoming genealogical events. Future events will be added on request. You can search for events by selecting either a location or a specific month, or you can download a text version of the complete calendar. Maintained by Mike St. Clair.

Calendar of Genealogical Events (Richard's):
http://www.compuology.com/events.htm

A calendar of genealogical events that is maintained by Richard S. Wilson. It contains mostly California and major national events. It also contains an index that takes you to the month and year you are interested in. Future events will be added upon request.

Cool Site of the Month for Genealogists:
http://www.cogensoc.org/cgs/cgs-cool.htm

What is a Cool Site? Cool sites are chosen for one or more of the following reasons: Previously undiscovered or not widely known to Web genealogists, an example of good genealogical work, useful or valuable information for genealogists. This site is updated each month with more cool sites.

Family Chronicle -Top Ten Genealogy Websites Nominees:
http://www.familychronicle.com/webpicks.htm

Family Chronicle surveyed experienced Web surfers to determine which of the Web's thousands of genealogy sites are not to be missed. They were particularly interested in discovering the "hidden gems"—little-known sites with a lot to offer. They recently had more than 185 top genealogy sites listed here.

Family Forum:
http://members.aol.com/familyserv/website/frmst1.htm

This site provides links to other genealogy sites on the Web and is an inexpensive site for genealogy vendors to advertise, as well as a site to search and store family data.

The Genealogy Home Page:
http://www.genhomepage.com/full.html

This site contains links to a pretty complete listing of various genealogy related sites.

Genealogy Resources on the Internet:
http://members.aol.com/johnf14246/gen_use.html

A listing of various genealogy related sites including: mailing lists, FTP sites, Telnet sites, Gopher sites, e-mail sites, Web and other sites.

Other Genealogy Sites:
http://www.afn.org/~afn09444/genealog/gensites.html

Another listing of genealogy sites on the Internet.

GenWeb.Net:
http://www.genweb.net/

GenWeb.Net is a domain setup to host genealogy and history Web pages. You can write them and they will set up space for a Web site for you at no cost. You are also welcome to set up a home page that will link to your web pages on another server.

Richard Wilson's Home Page:
http://www.compuology.com/richard/

Richard S. Wilson's personal home page. This site contains family histories and examples of at least five different methods of publishing your genealogical data on the Web. It also has a link to his calendar of genealogical events page.

Richard's "Other Genealogy Web Sites" page:
http://www.compuology.com/otherweb.htm

This site has links to many sites of genealogical interest on the Internet. It also has links to search engines and "people finder" sites. In fact, it currently contains links to all of the sites listed in this book.

What's Really New in WWW Genealogy Pages:
http://www.genhomepage.com/really_new.html

This page has links to sites of genealogical interest on the Internet. Many new links are added daily. Links date back to October 17, 1996.

Netiquette

Dear Emily Postnews:
http://www.clari.net/brad/emily.html

Emily Postnews, foremost authority on proper net behavior, gives her advice on how to act on the net. This is a very entertaining Netiquette site.

Netiquette:
http://www.in.on.ca/tutorial/netiquette.html

This book was the first in-print trade book (that we know of) to be offered in an online edition for the Worldwide Web. The entire book, from front cover to back cover, is available for instant purchase on the Bookport server. The online edition is virtually identical to the bound book that is sold in bookstores throughout the United States and Canada. Each page in the World Wide Web edition corresponds with a page in the bound book.

Netiquette Home Page, Published by Albion:
http://www.albion.com/netiquette/index.html

"Netiquette" is network etiquette – the do's and don'ts of online communication. Netiquette covers both common courtesy online and the informal "rules of the road" for cyberspace. This page provides links to both summary and detail information about Netiquette for your browsing pleasure.

Genealogy Megasites

Best Websites for Helping Genealogists:
http://www.nagara.org/clearinghouse/summer_97/kemp.html

A Web page set up by Thomas J. Kemp of the Special Collections Department, University of South Florida Library, Tampa Campus, *<tomkemp@lib.usf.edu>*.

Chance's Genealogy:
http://www.eskimo.com/~chance/

A list of genealogy mail lists, newsgroups, and special home pages. This is an alphabetical list of groups on the Internet that may be of value to genealogists.

Cyndi's List of Genealogy Sites on the Internet:
http://www.cyndislist.com/

One of the biggest and best sites for genealogy links, with more than 29,350 links categorized and cross-referenced in more than 90 categories (and growing rapidly).

Genealogy Gateway™ to the Web:
http://www.polaris.net/~legend/genalogy.htm

The **Genealogy Gateway™** is a genealogy and history listing service that now exceeds 16,000 links categorized by subject areas. There are now 12 "gateways" online and it is still growing. They are also beginning a "genealogy cooperative." Two examples of this are the "Gateway to Scotland" (under development) and the "Gateway to Obits" (a one-of-a-kind, on-line, 140 Newspaper Obit Search pages). By cooperative agreements with the University of Edinburgh in Scotland, and with Paul Peterson and Bruce Remick, they are able to utilize their resources to provide the gateway services.

Genealogy - The Mining Company:
http://genealogy.miningco.com/

This site contains links to many genealogy sites, a calendar of events, articles, new and genealogy chat sessions.

Genealogy Online:
http://genealogy.emcee.com/

This site contains links to archives and services that are available from Genealogy Online by Michael Cooley.

Helm's Genealogy Toolbox:
http://genealogy.tbox.com/

The Toolbox consists of links to genealogical information currently on the Internet. The Genealogy Toolbox contains a few new resources to aid users. The first is a search engine that allows users to find resources on their site in a quick and efficient way. An index to the entire site can be accessed from the main Toolbox page. Users can also see the entire Toolbox site at a glance by accessing the Genealogy Toolbox Site Map. Another resource is an "all-in-one" search section that allows users to search many different sites without having to go to those sites individually.

Janyce's Root Diggin' Dept.:
http://www.janyce.com/gene/rootdig.html

A very good listing of genealogy related pages on the Web. She has more than 1,500 links on the numerous pages of RootDig - worth the wait. The page is broken down into 18 different topics (departments). There is a great section for new people on the Web and many good genealogical links.

Library and Archives Resources:
http://www.dcn.davis.ca.us/~vctinney/archives.htm

A listing of links to archives, historical photographs, manuscripts, rare books, repositories of primary sources for the research scholar. It also contains links to genealogy on the Web and Salt Lake City LDS Family History Center information.

My Virtual Reference Desk - Genealogy:
http://www.refdesk.com/factgene.html

A Web page set up by Bob Drudge. This page contains information on atlas - maps, beginner's guides, biography / Who's Who, databases, dictionaries, electronic texts, encyclopedias, genealogy, government, grammar / style, history, Internet, law, libraries, misc., phone book, population, postal, science, thesaurus, time - date, weights - measures, world religions, and WWW Virtual Library.

Richard Eastman's Genealogy Forum on CompuServe®:
http://ourworld.compuserve.com/homepages/roots/

CompuServe's Genealogy Forum can supply you with the information you are looking for in a manner you can use quickly and easily. Many genealogy sources are available on CompuServe itself. And there are pointers to hundreds of other genealogy sources on the Internet.

Searchable Genealogy Links:
http://www.bc1.com/users/sgl/

These pages provide a comprehensive listing of original genealogical data that can be found on the Internet in the categories of African-American; Australia & New Zealand; Canada; Europe & Asia; General; Hispanic; Jewish; and U.S.A. The focus is on genealogy material that can be accessed without leaving your chair: names, dates, and places, primarily. It is, essentially, a compilation of links and resources that you may find useful in searching your family history on-line. They do not link genealogy pages that only give you a reference which you then need to write to in order to receive the "real" information. They also avoid linking pages devoted to only one (or a few) surnames or GEDCOMs.

TIC:

http://www.tic.com/gen.html

Texas Internet Consulting's Genealogical WWW Pages has links to many genealogy sites, sorted by category.

Yahoo!'s Genealogy Page:

http://www.yahoo.com/Arts/Humanities/History/Genealogy/

Links to many genealogy related pages. Don't forget to use Yahoo!'s (site specific) search engine to find other sections on Yahoo! with genealogy-related links.

Ethnic and Special Interest Sites

Acadian Genealogy Home Page:
http://www.acadian.org/

A genealogical page which includes complete details on the historical nonprofit "In Search of Our Acadian Roots" CD-ROM Project. There are also links to genealogy newsgroups, Acadian, Canadian, and French genealogy-related Web sites, as well as a large genealogy-related "Hot List" on the Web.

Afrigeneas Page:
http://www.msstate.edu/Archives/History/afrigen/

Afrigeneas is a mailing list focused on genealogical research and resources in general and on African ancestry in particular. This Web page serves as a focal point for information about African-ancestored families and for pointers to genealogical sources worldwide. Each of us may provide information to this collection. This page contains many great African American links and resources.

American Civil War Home page:
http://sunsite.utk.edu/civil-war/

The American Civil War Home page gathers together in one place hyperlinks to the most useful identified electronic files about the American Civil War (1861-1865). The page opens a gateway to the Internet's multi-formatted resources about what is arguably the seminal event in American history.

Cherokee National Historical Society:
http://www.Powersource.com/powersource/heritage/

In 1963, a group of distinguished Cherokees founded the Cherokee National Historical Society, a private nonprofit corporation designed to preserve the history and culture of the Cherokee people—past, present, and future.

Church of the Brethren - History & Genealogy:
http://www.cob-net.org/genhis.htm

Web site for the Church of the Brethren Network of Genealogy & History resources. Their Web site is divided into four sections: church records, miscellaneous lists, other genealogical Web sites, and libraries having genealogical archives. There are also additional Brethren online resources. Take the opportunity to learn about your Brethren ancestors.

Civil War Battle Summaries:
http://www2.cr.nps.gov/abpp/battles/tvii.htm

Part of·the National Park Services' American Battlefield Protection Program. Some 10,500 armed conflicts, ranging from major battles to minor skirmishes, occurred during the Civil War. The Civil War Sites Advisory Commission (CWSAC) identified 384 conflicts (3.7%) as the war's principal battles based on each conflict's historic significance. This site contains facts about these important battles.

Dead People Server:
http://www.city-net.com/~lmann/dps/

This is a fun and interesting site. The Dead People Server is simply a list of interesting celebrities who are, or might plausibly be, dead, including those who have been spaced, with information as to who has really "Rung Down the Curtain" and "Joined the Choir Invisible" and who's just resting. "Interesting" in the previous sentence means "I felt like putting them on this list."

Flags Of The World:
http://fotw.digibel.be/flags/

Flags Of The World (FOTW) is a Web site devoted to vexillology. Here you can read more than 1,500 pages and view more than 2,500 images about flags. The site is fed with news and images posted to FOTW mailing list and with other contributions. The contributors and the Editorial Staff work at FOTW freely. The contents of these pages are freely offered to the Internet community.

"Lutheran Roots" Genealogy Exchange:
http://www.aal.org/lutheran_roots/

Web page of the "Lutheran Roots" Genealogy Exchange, sponsored by Aid Association for Lutherans (AAL). This Web site consists of two sections: the Lutheran Roots Family Registry which allows others to more clearly see your family name, and the Lutheran Roots Genealogy Message Board where you can ask more broad-topic genealogy questions or share research tips. This site is especially helpful if you know that your ancestors were Lutheran or had some connection with a Lutheran church.

JewishGen: The Home of Jewish Genealogy:
http://www.jewishgen.org/

JewishGen®, Inc. is a primary Internet resource connecting researchers of Jewish genealogy worldwide. Its most popular components are the JewishGen Discussion Group, the JewishGen Family Finder (a database of over 70,000 surnames and towns), the comprehensive directory of InfoFiles, and a variety of databases like the ShtetlSeeker.

Molineaux Diary Index:
http://www.augustana.edu/library/diar5.html

Augustana College Library has transcribed the index for the Molineaux Diary. It covers Civil War troop movements from May 1865 to June 1866. Actual digitized diary pages can be viewed online.

NAVA-Flags of Native American Peoples of the U.S.:
http://www.nava.org/

The North American Vexillological Association (NAVA) is one of the oldest vexillological associations in the world. This is their official "Home Page." Vexillology is the study of flags.

Notable Women Ancestors:
http://members.aol.com/samcasey/ancestors/nw.html

There have been many famous (and infamous) women throughout history. There have also been thousands of lesser known women whose roles in history have often been overlooked. As every good genealogist also knows, there are an even greater number of women who, while possibly not contributing anything historically significant, nonetheless managed to lead very interesting lives. This Web page has been designed with all of these notable women in mind, offering both historical and genealogical information about them, as well as an occasional amusing anecdote.

The Political Graveyard:
http://www.potifos.com/tpg/index.html

A Web site indicating where dead politicians are buried, organized by state. They include great descriptions of local cemeteries.

Pony Express Home Page:
http://users.ccnet.com/~xptom/welcome.html

Ranked among the most remarkable fetes to come out of the American West, the Pony Express was in service from April 1860 to November 1861. Its primary mission was to deliver mail and news between St. Joseph, Missouri and San Francisco, California. This site contains extensive information about the Pony Express.

WWII U.S. Veterans Web Site:
http://ww2.vet.org/

The World War II U.S. Veterans Web site. This Internet Web site is dedicated to the millions of men and women from the United States who made the ultimate sacrifice for the good of free people everywhere.

Foreign Genealogy Research Sites

Carpatho-Rusyn Knowledge Base:
http://www.carpatho-rusyn.org/

This site is brought to you by genealogists Greg Gressa & Megan Smolenyak, and by the contributions of their readers, many organizations, and author friends. This site provides information pertaining to Carpatho-Rusyn culture, history, genealogy, etc., as well as other Web sites of similar interest. Their long term goal is to develop this site into an electronic knowledge base for the benefit of Carpatho-Rusyns worldwide who wish to learn more about their culture.

Czech Info Center - Find a Czech Ancestor:
http://www.muselik.com/cac/

If you are trying to find out more information about your family roots in the Czech Republic, this is the place for you. There is a **fee** to post a query on this site, but you can try it out for free for 14 days! Your posting may not exceed 5 lines of text. You can also read the current listings for free. The queries are listed in both the English and Czech languages.

Database of Irish On-Line Resources - Genealogy:
http://njd.ucg.ie/cgi-bin/irlnet-showdir/Genealogy?mode=&smagic=

This is a searchable database of many Irish genealogy resources that are available on the World Wide Web.

DBI-LINK - German Libraries:
http://www.dbilink.de/en/

DBI-LINK offers access to supraregional library-catalogues, table-of-contents, literature and index-databases with holdings locations of approximately 3,000 German libraries. Connected to the databases is a comfortable document-order-system enabling users to place online-orders subsequently to a title search. At the moment twenty one German libraries accept online-orders via DBI-LINK.

Federation of East European Family History Societies:
http://feefhs.org/

An 108.6 megabyte site of genealogical data with an eleven megabyte "Web Site Index" that has been created by their Web site full text search engine indexer. You can use it to find a hypertext index to any of 212,196 unique words in the 3,633 files on their Web site. This "site specific" search engine is re-indexed anytime something is added, changed, or deleted from their Web site.

Gary Kemper's German Resources:
http://users.deltanet.com/users/gkemper/ger.html

This site contains a wide variety of German resources that are available online, including: miscellaneous Germany resources, WWW servers in Germany, German search engines and indexes, book search engines, German book publishers, publishers and bookstores, reference books, newspapers, and magazines.

Genealogy and Poland - A Guide:
http://members.aol.com/genpoland/genpolen.htm

Millions of people all around the world trace their roots to the territory of present-day Poland. Their ancestors might have been of Polish, German, Jewish or other ethnic backgrounds and they might have belonged to the Roman Catholic, Greek Catholic, Lutheran, Orthodox, Calvinist or Mennonite Churches, or professed Judaism. This guide is designed to help their descendants research their family's history dating back to different times and places in contemporary Poland.

Germans from Russia Heritage Society:
http://grhs.com/

Home page of the Germans From Russia Heritage Society. The society was founded on January 9, 1971 at Bismarck, ND under the name North Dakota Historical Society of Germans from Russia (NDHSGR). On July 14, 1979, the membership, by popular vote, changed the name to Germans from Russia Heritage Society (GRHS).

German Genealogy Home Page:
http://www.genealogy.com/

This page provides links to German genealogy resources on the Internet.

Italian Genealogical Group:
http://www.italiangen.org/

Web site of the Italian Genealogical Group (IGG). They bring together individuals researching their Italian genealogy. They have links to some very good Italian Web sites as well as some online information.

Luxembourg Gazetteer of villages and towns Online:
http://www.igd-leo.lu/igd-leo/onomastics/villages/villages.html

A gazetteer of Luxembourg villages and towns is now available on the World Wide Web. Luxembourg place names have the peculiarity of sometimes having three different versions depending on if the French, German, or Luxembourg Version was used. This can be very confusing for a genealogist who discovers a Luxembourg place name in a record but cannot find that name on the Luxembourg map. This site is an answer to that problem.

New South Wales Registry (Australia):
http://www.agd.nsw.gov.au/bdm/

The *New South Wales Registry of Births, Deaths and Marriages* records all births, deaths and marriages occurring in New South Wales (Australia) and provides documentation to individuals to help establish a range of legal entitlements. The registry collects statistical data for governments and other organizations, and performs civil marriages.

Poland - Guide to the State Archives:
http://darkstar.ci.uw.edu.pl/archiwa/books/ap25.html

A guide to the holdings of the State Archives in Radom. It contains short information about each fond: the title, dates of creation, size, brief administrative history of the creators, characteristic of the contents and bibliography.

Public Record Office (PRO):
http://www.pro.gov.uk/

This is the Web site of the Public Record Office (PRO). They are the national archives of England, Wales and the United Kingdom.

Scottish Roots:
http://www.ScotWeb.co.uk/ScotRoots/

This is a **fee-based** ancestral research service. This site contains no online data. However, if you know the name and date of an ancestor who was born, married, or died in Scotland, preferably after 1855, a full search can be arranged.

Scots Origins:
http://www.origins.net/GRO/

The Scots Origins database is an online pay-per-view **FEE** database that contains fully searchable indexes of the GRO(S) index to births/baptisms and banns/marriages from the Old Parish Registers dating from 1553 to 1854, plus it contains the indexes to births, deaths and marriages from 1855 to 1897.

South & West Wales Genealogical Index:
http://members.aol.com/swalesidx/

This is a large index to marriages, births, baptisms, wills, and other genealogical information available to the family historian in South Wales. They also have St. Catherine's House marriages during 1837-1852. Eventually they will have indexes of all the marriages for Glamorgan & Carmarthenshire from 1754-1952 and Pembrokeshire & Cardiganshire from 1813-1952.

Tracing your Scottish Ancestry:
http://www.geo.ed.ac.uk/home/scotland/genealogy.html

This is a collection of resources designed to assist those wishing to trace their Scottish ancestry. They have tried to include all new major Scottish resources which will help you find out more about where your ancestors came from.

UK and Ireland:
http://midas.ac.uk/genuki/big/

This Web site lists newsgroups and resources for England, Ireland, Scotland, Wales, Channel Islands, and the Isle of Man. This page provides pointers to these six areas, plus information which relates to the UK and Ireland as a whole.

Language Aids

Dictionaries & Etc:
http://www.cis.hut.fi/~peura/dictionaries.html

This Web site contains links to various dictionaries and other useful resources.

Genealogy Dictionary:
http://w3g.med.uni-giessen.de/CGB/genetxt/buzzwo.rds

Dick Eastman's genealogy dictionary listing. This file contains many of the common "buzzwords," terminology and legal words found in genealogy work.

Genealogy Dictionary:
http://www.electriciti.com/~dotts/diction.html

Have you ever come across a word you don't know when doing your genealogy? Check here for those special word meanings.

German Translation Service > Old Script:
http://www.win.bright.net/~jakeschu/welcome.html

Their specialties are church records, civil and military documents, and letters in the Old German Script.

OneLook Dictionaries:
http://www.onelook.com/

This site is a metasearch dictionary containing information from 287 dictionaries.

Online Dictionaries and Translators:
http://rivendel.com/~ric/resources/dictionary.html

A Web site with language dictionaries and translators for many different languages.

Online Grammars:
http://www.bucknell.edu/~rbeard/grammars.html

This page maintains links with on-line grammars of as many languages as can be found on the Web. It includes all types of grammars: reference grammars, learning grammars, and historical grammars.

Travlang's Translating Dictionaries:
http://dictionaries.travlang.com/

Dictionaries are available for online use to translate from English ⇨ German, English ⇨ Dutch, English ⇨ French, English ⇨ Spanish, English ⇨ Danish, English ⇨ Finnish, English ⇨ Portuguese, English ⇨ Afrikaans, and English ⇨ Esperanto.

A Web of On-line Dictionaries:
http://www.bucknell.edu/~rbeard/diction.html

This site is linked to more than 500 dictionaries of over 140 different languages.

Genealogical Software Sites

Ancestral Quest Home Page:
http://www.ancquest.com/

This is the Web site of Ancestral Quest, an exciting Windows program that makes it possible for anyone to do genealogy! It is easy-to-learn and fun to use. Ancestral Quest is the only genealogy software program written for Windows to be built on the PAF 2.31 database. The PAF (Personal Ancestral File®) genealogy program is an industry standard for DOS computers. This program is not yet compatible with the PAF 3.0 database, an update to this program is expected in Fall of 1998.

Ann Turner's GEDCOM Utilities:
http://members.aol.com/APTurner/gedutils.htm

This page contains the GEDWRAP utility for converting notes from the older GEDCOM standard to the newer 5.5 GEDCOM standard. Ann Turner is currently working on developing a more comprehensive package called GEDUTILS.

Corel Family Tree Suite: See Family Heritage

Cumberland Family Tree:
http://www.cf-software.com/

The Cumberland Family Tree for Windows DELUXE Package includes Cumberland Family Tree, Cumberland Diary for Windows, and Cumberland Family Photo Album for Windows. Only the CFT-Win is available as a 32-bit program; however, both the Diary and the Family Photo Album will run smoothly in the Windows 95/98 environment. You may download all three programs for testing.

Design Software:
http://www.dhc.net/~design/

Creators of specialized genealogy software that can help you organize your special genealogy records. They make Family Census Research, Family Marriage Research, and the Genealogical Cemetery Database.

Family Forest Software Home Page:
http://www.FamilyForest.com/

(Genealogy CD ROMs) Whether you are interested in searching for your ancestors or studying United States history, they invite you to take a closer look at the *Exploring a Family Forest* video, and the *Delaware Family Forest*, *Pittsburgh Family Forest* and *Founders & Patriots Family Forest* CD-ROMs.

Family Heritage Home Page:
http://www.mindscape.com/familyheritage/

Corel Family Tree Suite had been acquired by IMSI and re-named Family Heritage Deluxe. They have now been bought out by Mindscape.

Family Matters® Genealogy Software:
http://members.aol.com/matterware/index.html

Family Matters® is a shareware genealogy program written expressly for Windows by Ray Nicklas. It now creates Web pages.

Family Origins Home Page:
http://www.parsonstech.com/software/famorig.html

Your family counts on you to preserve its history. Now you can count on the new Family Origins 6.0 to help you create a detailed family tree that is sure to be enjoyed today and for generations to come. It can now create great looking Web pages.

Family Tracker Home Page:
http://www.surfutah.com/web/famtrak/famtrak.html

Family Tracker is a Windows 3.1-based genealogy program designed to aid in the data acquisition of genealogy related information. It has a unique front end interface which allows easy access to individual records by a simple double click. The pedigree branches may be expanded and collapsed by clicking on the expansion/collapsing icon.

Family Tree Maker Home Page:
https://store1-4.broderbund.com/products/fs-home.html

Broderbund's home page for its Family Tree Maker™ Deluxe software. FTM includes: ancestor and descendant trees, kinship reports, birthday and anniversary calendars, hundreds of reports, family group sheets and individual fact sheets, scrapbook pages, mailing labels, cards and name tags and family books. It can create Web pages, but **only** for use on their Web Site. It is now available for Macintosh computers.

Family Tree House:
http://www.usaafter.com/

The FamilyTree House™ Web site of AFTER™, the Association for FamilyTree Enrollment and Registry. This site offers free family tree software on-line. You can build your FamilyTree House in real time; no downloading is required. Membership in AFTER is free. Once you are a member of AFTER, you create and register your own online FamilyTree. And because it is online, you can enlist the help of other family members by giving them your personal access code to allow them to fill in the missing branches.

Family Tree Maker Online Home Page:
http://www.familytreemaker.com/

Family Tree Maker's online site with links to personal Web pages published on their site.

FamilySearch FAQ:
http://www.utw.com/~tornado/

This FAQ site attempts to answer many commonly asked questions (that have appeared in various genealogy newsgroups) about FamilySearch, and to clear misconceptions found in the genealogy community about this software, its availability, and its use in general.

GEDCOM Utilities Page:
http://www.rootsweb.com/~gumby/ged.html

A Web page with GEDCOM utility programs, set up by Randy Winch.

GEN-BOOK Home Page:
http://www.foothill.net/~genbook/

Generate a GENealogy BOOK from PAF or Ancestral Quest to be put into WordPerfect or Microsoft Word. A GED-BOOK version has been added for use with GEDCOM files so that now you can generate a book from almost any genealogy program, including the new PAF 3.0 program. GEN-BOOK and GED-BOOK give you a pleasingly large number of options when creating your family history book.

Gene:
http://www.ics.uci.edu/~eppstein/gene/

Gene is a shareware Macintosh genealogy database management program written by Diana and David Eppstein. You can use Gene to store family data and notes, draw and print family trees and pedigree charts, show how different people are related, or browse the database by clicking on names in cards and trees. Gene is capable of handling complicated databases with thousands of names, multiple marriages and divorces, adoptions, illegitimate children, and intermarriage between relatives.

Genealogy Software Springboard:
http://www.toltbbs.com/~kbasile/software.html

This site was created to help fellow genealogists review genealogy programs. The pros and cons of the programs have been submitted by the users of these programs, not just the features the developers outline for you. These personal insights give a better view of the programs' abilities and functions. This is not an attempt to list all software programs available. It is a review of the more widely used programs. If you are interested in shareware programs, there are currently a few listed here.

Generations:
http://www.sierra.com/titles/genealogy/

Formerly *Reunion for Windows.* Sierra Software recently bought this version of Reunion from Lester Productions. This program is especially flexible when it comes to creating and customizing charts and reports.

Heritage Genealogy Software:
http://www.eskimo.com/%7Egrandine/heritage.html

Heritage Genealogy Software is a Macintosh genealogy program.

KINWRITE Plus:
http://www2.dtc.net/~ldbond/

KINWRITE Plus is a product which merges the capabilities of *Kinwrite* and *Kinpublish*. It allows you to publish a book from PAF 2.31.

Legacy Family Tree:
http://www.LegacyFamilyTree.com/

Home page of the new *Legacy Family Tree* software. This site claims their software is comprehensive and easy-to-use. You can take a guided tour at this site and try their free demo. This is a very full-featured program that is constantly adding even more features. They are very responsive to fix reported bugs and add requested features.

Louis Kessler's Genealogical Program Link:
http://www.concentric.net/~Lkessler/gplinks.shtml

One person's listing of the genealogy programs that are available. It also includes their opinion of which programs are the best.

Macintosh Genealogy Programs:
http://www.cyberenet.net/~gsteiner/macgsfaq/macprog.html

This site lists many of the genealogy programs that are available for the Macintosh computer.

Our Family Tree:
http://www.alphasoftware.com/

This is the Web site of Alpha software, makers of *Our Family Tree*. Use *Our Family Tree* to organize and document all your findings, then display your ancestors by creating beautiful family trees that can be printed in different colors and sizes, including posters. This program includes a Federal Government database of over 55 million names.

PAF Review:
http://www.genealogy.org/~paf/

An electronic newsletter covering utilities for genealogists who use PAF or GEDCOM. PAF Review describes more than two hundred utilities and includes other related material such as a list of PAF User Groups, you can download shareware utilities from this site.

Reunion Home Page:
http://www.LeisterPro.com/

Web page of Leister Productions, Inc., developer of Reunion—family tree software for Macintosh. Reunion helps you to document, store, and display genealogy information - names, dates, facts, plenty of notes, sources of information, and digitized pictures.

The Gold Bug:
http://www.goldbug.com/

A small company providing historical information and software for genealogical research, academic study, or to satisfy your curiosity. They have a large selection of reproductions of early maps of the United States, Europe and the world going back to the 16th century. They are the makers of AniMap Plus U.S. County Boundary Historical Atlas software for Windows, designed to aid in genealogical research.

The Master Genealogist (TMG):
http://www.whollygenes.com/

TMG is an excellent genealogical database program. It has a very easy-to-use interface that makes it a cinch for beginners to use, with enough power underneath to satisfy the most experienced computer genealogist. TMG is written by Wholly Genes, Inc. TMG provides many advanced research features.

Ultimate Family Tree:
http://www.uftree.com/

Palladium Interactive software recently bought out Commsoft, the maker of Roots V. They discontinued the "Family Gathering" and "Roots" programs and have released this new product, designed help to set new higher standards for genealogical computing software.

Win-Family Home Page:
http://www.jamodat.dk/winfammain.htm

Win-Family is a genealogy software program for both the beginner and the more experienced genealogist. This program is user friendly, yet it still contains a lot of functions for the more experienced as well. The data entered can be presented in various forms like suns, trees, statistics and many different types of printouts.

Genealogical and Historical Societies Online

Association of Professional Genealogists (APG):
http://www.apgen.org/~apg/

Web page for the APG, a professional association for all genealogists supporting high standards in the field of genealogy. Formed in 1979 by nineteen genealogists to promote standards and ethics in the genealogical field, they currently have more than 1,000 members worldwide.

Board for Certification of Genealogists:
http://www.genealogy.org/~bcg/

Since its founding in 1964, the Board for Certification of Genealogists, independent of any society, has stood for the highest standards of competence and ethics. The Board views genealogical practice as a profession or hobby that requires training and advanced skills. It defines a client as anyone who receives the benefit of the genealogist's work, regardless of whether or not a fee is paid for that benefit. Individuals certified in genealogy, like those in any profession, are expected to pass qualifying examinations.

California Historical Society Home Page:
http://www.calhist.org/index.html

As the state's official historical society, they hold extensive materials about California's rich history. Their Web site is still young but growing and it primarily provides "content" for researchers. They invite you to visit their headquarters at 678 Mission Street in the South of Market/Yerba Buena area of San Francisco.

California Genealogical Society:
http://members.aol.com/calgensoc/home/home.htm

The California Genealogical Society, founded in 1898, is the oldest genealogical society in the State of California. Their purpose is to help people trace and compile their family histories. They maintain a library, gather and preserve vital records, and provide education through meetings, seminars and workshops.

California State Genealogical Alliance (CSGA):
http://www.dcn.davis.ca.us/go/feefhs/csga/frg-csga.html

Founded in October 1982, the California State Genealogical Alliance serves as a statewide association of independent genealogical societies, individuals, and nonprofit organizations, such as libraries. It was organized to meet the need for a statewide effort to accomplish major goals of benefit to all genealogists.

Computer Genealogy Society of San Diego:
http://www.cgssd.org/

The CGSSD is an association of people using personal computers in the pursuit of their genealogical research. The computer, coupled with genealogy software, allows you to better manage and share the family history information you have gathered. The computer allows you to print out your research information in many formats and share it with others. Computers can also help with genealogy research by providing access to databases, CD-ROM data files, and the Internet.

East Tennessee Historical Society:
http://www.korrnet.org/eths/

The East Tennessee Historical Society traces its roots to the *East Tennessee Historical and Antiquarian Society*, founded in 1834 by distinguished Tennessee historian Dr. J.G.M. Ramsey. The East Tennessee Historical Society was revived in 1925 with its headquarters in Lawson McGhee Library. The Society and the Library have enjoyed a long history of working together to preserve books and historic manuscripts for the study of Tennessee history.

The Federation of Family History Societies:
http://www.vellum.demon.co.uk/genuki/FFHS/

FFHS was formed in 1974 as a result of the growing interest in the study of family history. Since then its membership has grown to almost 200 societies throughout the world including national, regional and one-name groups. Its principal aims are to co-ordinate and assist the work of societies or other bodies that are interested in Family History, Genealogy, and Heraldry and to foster mutual co-operation and regional projects in these subjects.

FEEFHS Index Page:
http://feefhs.org/masteri.html

This is the Master Index to the Federation of East European Family History Societies (FEEFHS) Web site. The new full text search engine at this Web site has decreased the use of this index, but has not decreased its importance for those who want to understand how the FEEFHS Web site is organized and how to find related information more quickly.

FGS (Federation of Genealogical Societies):
http://www.fgs.org/~fgs/

The Federation of Genealogical Societies, founded in 1976, has three major purposes: serving the needs of its member societies, providing products and services needed by member societies, and marshaling the resources of its member organizations.

Genealogical Websites of Societies & CIGS:
http://genealogy.org/PAF/www/gwsc/

This Web site is maintained by Mike St. Clair. GWSC has links to nearly 1,000 societies and CIG home pages. This growth required him to put a separate link for the Canadian societies to reduce the size of the international page.

GENTECH Information:
http://www.gentech.org/~gentech/

GENTECH, Inc. is an independent, nonprofit organization chartered in the state of Texas to educate genealogists in the use of technology for gathering, storing, sharing and evaluating their research.

International Internet Genealogical Society:
http://www.iigs.org/

They envision their organization as a key to worldwide genealogy. For the most part, they want to help others acquire and store information in their own repositories, whether by funding, by sheer volume of volunteer manpower, or simply through technical advice. Their goal is to help genealogists worldwide to have interactive access to all the information placed online no matter where geographically it may be physically located.

National Genealogical Society Home Page:
http://www.ngsgenealogy.org/

NGS is a national organization with more than 15,000 members nationwide. Although most of its members are individuals, its institutional members include genealogical and historical societies, family organizations, libraries, and other organizations.

New England Historic Genealogical Society Home Page:
http://www.nehgs.org/

The New England Historic Genealogical Society (NEHGS) has the largest and oldest genealogical library in the world. The NEHGS has more than 16,000 members worldwide.

Irish Family History Foundation:
http://www.mayo-ireland.ie/roots.htm

The Irish Family History Foundation is the coordinating body for a network of government approved genealogical research centers in the Republic of Ireland (Eire) and in Northern Ireland. They have computerized tens of millions of Irish ancestral records of different types. They have many records available, but charge a fee for searches.

National Society Daughters of the American Revolution:
http://www.dar.org/

Incorporated by an Act of Congress in 1896, the National Society Daughters of the American Revolution (NSDAR) is a non-profit, non-political, volunteer service organization with nearly 180,000 women in some 3,000 chapters in each of the fifty states, the District of Columbia, Australia, Canada, France, Mexico, the United Kingdom and Japan. The Society was founded in Washington, D.C. on October 11, 1890 and has celebrated more than 100 years of service to the nation.

National Society Sons of the American Revolution:
http://www.sar.org/

In keeping with the educational goals and objectives of the National Society Sons of the American Revolution (NSSAR), this web site is designed to "perpetuate the memory of those who, by their services or sacrifices during the war of the American Revolution, achieved the independence of the American People."

North San Diego County Genealogy Society Home Page:
http://www.compuology.com/nsdcgs/

North San Diego County Genealogy Society (NSDCGS) was formed in 1968 by a group of North County San Diego genealogists living in the Carlsbad area. Today the genealogy collection in the Carlsbad Library has grown to more than 40,000 volumes and is still increasing due to the generosity of the 650 members of the society.

Orange County California Genealogical Society:
http://www.occgs.com/

World Wide Web page of the Orange County California Genealogical Society (OCCGS) based at the Huntington Beach, California Central Library. They have 700+ members.

Questing Heirs Genealogical Society, Inc. Home Page:
http://www.compuology.com/questing/

The society was founded in June, 1969 for the purpose of collecting, preserving, and publishing data relating to genealogy. Meetings are held the third Sunday of each month at 1:15 P.M. All members receive the monthly newsletter.

RAND Genealogy Club:
http://www.rand.org:80/personal/Genea/

They were formed by a group of several Rand employees who share the hobby of tracing family trees. This site has a free searchable database and excellent links to other areas on the Internet.

San Diego Genealogical Society:
http://www.genealogy.org/~sdgs/

The society was founded in 1946 by Mrs. Alicia P. Mayer and a small group of people interested in genealogy. Mrs. Mayer, the first president, stated the main purposes of the society are "to promote general interest in the related fields of genealogy, history and heraldry," to assist members with their research, and to establish a genealogical library.

Santa Barbara Genealogical Society Home Page:
http://www.compuology.com/sbarbara/

They promote study and research in genealogy by providing assistance for those interested in pursuing their family history. The genealogy collection in the SBCGS Library has grown to more than 4,000 volumes.

Silicon Valley PAF Users Group:
http://www.genealogy.org/~svpafug/

The Silicon Valley PAF Users Group (SVPUG) is recognized worldwide as a leader in computer genealogy. More than 1,800 members strong, it is a nonprofit organization focused on education and development of computer genealogy methods. This site contains information about the group, the GenWeb Project, and related genealogy topics. It contains links to genealogy areas on the Web.

South Orange County California Genealogy Society:
http://www.genealogy.org/~soccgs/

Home page for the South Orange County California Genealogy Society (SOCCGS), including back issues of their newsletters, and projects their members are working on. They even have an online application for membership.

Southern California Chapter, APG:
http://www.compuology.com/sccapg/

This is the home page for the Southern California Chapter of the Association of Professional Genealogists (SCCAPG). They are a local chapter of the Association of Professional Genealogists (APG).

Southern California Genealogical Society (SCGS):
http://www.cwire.com/scgs/

The Southern California Genealogical Society was organized January 1964 to foster interest in genealogy, preserve genealogical materials, and train researchers in effective and accurate techniques. They host the Southern California "Genealogical Jamboree" in Pasadena every year.

United States Internet Genealogical Society:
http://www.usigs.org/

The USIGS was developed as a result of discussions between several people trying once again to get the USGenWeb Project incorporated as a nonprofit organization. A suggestion was made during this time period that instead of trying to incorporate USGenWeb that a separate nonprofit organization should be formed that would support the total Internet genealogical community. That is the purpose of this society.

Utah Valley PAF Users Group:
http://www.genealogy.org/~uvpafug/

UV-PAF-UG is an organization of genealogists who use computers and Personal Ancestral File for record keeping. Although they meet in Provo, their members come from throughout Utah, from other states, even some from overseas. In addition to providing information about the group, over time this Web page may become a source of information on the bustling genealogy scene in central Utah. This site contains many genealogical links.

Whittier Area Genealogy Society (WAGS) Home Page:
http://www.compuology.com/wags/

They are based in Whittier, California. This site also includes information about their Computer Interest Group (CIG).

Library & Catalog Sites

Allen County Public Library Home Page:
http://www.acpl.lib.in.us/

The Allen County (Ft. Wayne, IN) Public Library World Wide Web home page contains general information about ACPL, an online catalog, links to Internet sites, library events, presentations and a search engine for ACPL's Web pages.

American Library Association Home Page:
http://www.ala.org/

The site contains ALA lists and discussion groups, frequently asked questions, links to library Web resources, and more.

Brigham Young University Libraries Info Network:
http://www.lib.byu.edu/

The Brigham Young University (BYU) Libraries Information Network World Wide Web Server. They encourage your comments and suggestions.

CARLweb - Library Catalog Site:
http://www.carl.org:1080/cweb1.html

CARLweb presents a seamless and simple gateway and navigation aid to the information universe. CARLweb was designed with a single, unified purpose; to support the library's mission to provide the most powerful access and retrieval possible to all of its users regardless of their skill level or the complexity of their information need.

Electric Library:
http://www.elibrary.com/

The Electric Library makes it possible to conduct real research over the Internet, using a deep database of reliable sources. With the Electric Library, any person can pose a question in plain English and launch a comprehensive, simultaneous search through numerous full-text newspapers, full-text magazines, maps, and photographs.

HYTEL (Library Catalogues on the World Wide Web):
http://library.usask.ca/hytelnet/

HYTELNET is the utility which gives an IBM-PC user instant-access to all Telnet-accessible library catalogs, FREE-NETS, BBSes, Gophers, WAIS, etc. This site includes library catalogs arranged geographically, and library catalogs arranged by vendor. You must use a Telnet program to access the catalogs.

The Internet Public Library:
http://ipl.sils.umich.edu/

This resource is the result of a great deal of time and hard work (not to mention late nights, maniacal laughter, and the occasional muttered death threat) on the part of a great many dedicated, talented people.

LDS Church Family History Centers:
http://www.lds.org/Family_History/Where_is.html

The Church of Jesus Christ of Latter-day Saints' Family History Library in Salt Lake City, Utah has one of the most impressive collections of genealogical material in the world. The Family History Library is **NOT ONLINE**. However, many of the resources of the Library are available through local Family History Centers throughout the world. This site has a complete list of all Family History Centers.

Library of Congress Home Page:
http://lcweb.loc.gov/homepage/lchp.html

The Library of Congress is using the World Wide Web to present
information about, and materials from, its collections over the Internet.
Find out what is new on the library's Web Site, or access any of the
following categories of information: about the library and the World
Wide Web; exhibits and events; services and publications; digital library
collections; LC online systems; congress and government; and indexes
to other World Wide Web services.

Library of Virginia Digital Collections:
http://image.vtls.com/

This site includes an online catalog, archives and manuscript database,
digitized Bible records, and the Virginia Colonial Records project.
Excellent finding aids online and exciting digitized primary records are
being added regularly.

Los Angeles Main Public Library:
http://www.lapl.org/

This site provides access to the Los Angeles Public Library Catalog. You
can use a graphical Web-based search OR you can open a text-based
Telnet session, if your Internet browser supports a Telnet application.
The catalog contains 1.2 million records representing the more than five
million library materials located at the library and in the sixty-six
branches of the library system. At this time, periodicals, newspapers,
corporate annual reports, patents, many government documents, and
photographs are **NOT** included in the catalog.

MELVYL System Welcome Page:
http://www.dla.ucop.edu/

The University of California's MELVYL library system was developed by the Division of Library Automation (DLA) at the UC Office of the President, in consultation with UC campuses. The system can search the UC union catalog (materials at all UC campuses, plus other locations), the California Academic Libraries List of Serials (periodical titles at California academic libraries), and other databases and Internet resources.

OCLC (Online Computer Library Center):
http://www.oclc.org/

OCLC is a nonprofit membership library computer service and research organization dedicated to the public for purposes of furthering access to the world's information, and reducing information costs.

Texas State Electronic Library:
http://link.tsl.state.tx.us/

The Texas State Electronic Library (TSEL) gives you the ability to ask a reference question, search dictionaries, find out about the weather, and other quick facts. You can search the book stacks, reference, electronic lists and news, print indexes and articles, Library of Congress and subject guides. They also have a search engine so you can search their entire site.

webCATS (Library Catalogues on the Web):
http://library.usask.ca/hywebcat/

This site contains a list of links to library catalogs that are available for access through the World Wide Web.

Map & Gazetteer Sites

Canadian Geographical Names:
http://GeoNames.NRCan.gc.ca/geonames.html

This site is an interactive and authoritative source of over 500,000 geographical names in Canada, which is maintained by the Canadian Permanent Committee on Geographical Names (CPCGN). By combining this server and the Canadian Geographical Names Data Base (CGNDB), they provide a simple reference service, which includes basic vocational information and maps that are easy to download. It's a popular source of information for researchers, genealogists, cartographers and students.

Gazetteer for Scotland:
http://www.geo.ed.ac.uk/~scotgaz/gazhome.htm

Part of an on-going project by the Department of Geography at the University of Edinburgh, this site will hold a comprehensive geographical database for Scotland, accessible via the World-Wide Web. The "Gazetteer for Scotland" is being designed in collaboration with the Royal Scottish Geographical Society as an enhancement to the well-known Gateway to Scotland Web site, implemented by Bruce Gittings at the University of Edinburgh.

Historical Ink:
http://members.aol.com/oldmapsne/

This site contains Old Maps of New York, Maine, Massachusetts, Rhode Island, New Hampshire, Vermont, and Connecticut Cities, Towns & Villages & Gazetteer Excerpts. These are **not** online, they are available for a **fee**.

Historical County Lines Site:
http://www.geocities.com/Heartland/2297/maps.htm

This site contains an animated presentation of the formation of the 48 contiguous states and the counties in those states. It also has maps showing the U.S. territorial expansion from 1775 to the present. It also has links to various maps sorted by state.

MapBlast!:
http://www.mapblast.com/

Use this site to locate a detailed street map from almost any street address in the United States, e-mail a map to somebody, or add a map to your home page by generating a HTML code fragment you can cut and paste (this is not as hard as it sounds).

MapQuest:
http://www.mapquest.com/

This site includes an interactive atlas, TripQuest, to help plan your trip and personalized maps. This site can even be used to find small towns in European countries, such as Poland.

Maps and Cartography Resources:
http://www.library.arizona.edu/users/mount/maps.html

This Web site was created by Jack Mount, the Science-Engineering Librarian at the University of Arizona Library. This page will give Web and some printed resources for cartography and maps to help you with your research. These Web pages deal with the subjects of Maps, Cartography, and Geographic Names.

My Virtual Reference Desk - Atlas and Maps:
http://www.refdesk.com/factmaps.html

A Web page set up by Bob Drudge. This page contains information on atlases and maps.

PCL Map Collection (Univ. of Texas):
http://www.lib.utexas.edu/Libs/PCL/Map_collection/Map_collection.html

The Perry-Castaneda Library Map Collection at the University of Texas at Austin has a very good map resources list. The site also includes maps of other areas in the world.

Proximus:
http://www.proximus.com/yahoo/

Create a map using a street address, an intersection, or a city and state. (U.S. addresses only.)

Rare Map Collection at the Hargrett Library:
http://scarlett.libs.uga.edu/darchive/hargrett/maps/maps.html

The more than 800 rare maps in the Hargrett Library at the University of Georgia Library span 500 years, from the sixteenth through the early twentieth century. They include works of the early cartographers such as Sebastain Munster, Gerard Mercator, and Willem Bleau.

TIGER Mapping Service:
http://tiger.census.gov/instruct.html

The Tiger Mapping Service Map Browser allows you to access TMS-generated maps. You can request maps by inputting the latitude and longitude of the place for which you want to generate a map.

U.S. Gazetteer:
http://tiger.census.gov/cgi-bin/gazetteer

This searchable gazetteer identifies places to view with the Tiger Map Server, and obtain census data from the 1990 Census Lookup server. You can search for places or counties by entering the name and state abbreviation (optional), or 5-digit zip code.

U.S. Geological Survey National Mapping Information:
http://www-nmd.usgs.gov/

The USGS, through its National Mapping Program, provides accurate and up-to-date cartographic data and information for the United States. They also have links to their other regional mapping centers.

U.S. Surname Distribution:
http://www.hamrick.com/names/

Are you curious where other people with your same last name (surname) live in the United States? Interested in genealogy? Just enter any surname into their form, and you will see a map of the United States showing the distribution of people with this surname within the 50 United States. This database contains 50,000 of the most common surnames in the United States.

U.S.G.S. - National Mapping Query Form:
http://www-nmd.usgs.gov/www/gnis/gnisform.html

Geographic Names Information System (GNIS) is an online database query form. A simple database query would be a search for information about a specific geographic feature by its name. For example, "List all features anywhere in the United States with names beginning with the word 'felder'," or "Identify features in TN with the name Cove Creek."

Genealogy Book Stores & Publishers

20th Century Direct:
http://www.20thcenturydirect.com/

20th Century Direct carries archival photo and scrapbook pages, available in an unmatched variety of page formats. They offer over 100 styles and colors of photo albums and scrapbooks.

Amazon Books:
http://www.amazon.com/

Although this is not exclusively a genealogy bookstore, it is the largest collection of books for sale in the world, via the Internet. They catalog more than 2.5 million books.

American Genealogical Lending Library (AGLL):
http://www.agll.com/

AGLL Genealogical Services is one of America's largest family history providers. They have thousands of genealogy products and services available, and they publish two genealogy magazines: the Genealogy Bulletin, and Heritage Quest. There is a search engine for searching their site.

Ancestry, Inc. Home Page:
http://www.ancestry.com/

Ancestry Inc. provides family history products and services, including books, periodicals, computer products, maps, charts, and professional research services. They invite you to their Web site to discover how Ancestry can help you learn about your ancestors.

Appleton's Books:
http://www.appletons.com/

Previously called Moobasi. For those of you who visited their site before, you may notice that the format has changed to improve the user-friendliness of this friendly genealogy book dealer's Web site.

Automated Research, Inc.™:
http://www.aricds.com/

Automated Research, Inc.™'s primary goal is to serve genealogists with the best possible research aids, resources, and sources for the computer. They carry a wide selection of genealogical compact discs.

Book Craftsman:
http://www.bookcraftsman.com/

It's almost a forgotten art. But, at The Book Craftsman, hand bookbinding and the rebuilding of old and valuable books continues in the quality and tradition of the past. Your memories can be preserved for generations to come. They can also bind your own family history book for you. They can bind in the quantity of books you desire. Your order can be as small as one book!

Broken Arrow Publishing:
http://clanhuston.com/

They can help you create a bound volume from your research. Reasonable rates and library standard binding, which meets the specifications of the Library Binding Institute.

Byron Sistler and Associates, Inc:
http://www.mindspring.com/~sistler/

They have sold genealogy books since 1968, including census records, wills, deeds, marriages, and more. Their catalog features over 900 genealogy titles covering records from Tennessee, Virginia, North Carolina, and Kentucky.

Census View:
http://www.galstar.com/~censusvu/

They sell actual census records on CD-ROM (not transcribed records or just an index—actual digitized images). Installation is not required for the following features: multiple print options; unlimited zoom, lighten, darken, invert; select by page number, use existing indexes; no membership fees.

Everton Publisher's Home Page:
http://www.everton.com/

This site contains Everton's Online Genealogical Helper, "Helping More People Find More Genealogy." It also contains information about research, genealogy software, and Internet resources.

Family Chronicle Magazine:
http://www.familychronicle.com/

Family Chronicle magazine is specially written for family researchers by people who share their interest in genealogy and family history. You may be interested in several unsolicited comments that readers have shared with them. Researchers may want to find out about Family Chronicle classifieds.

Frontier Press:
http://www.doit.com/frontier/frontier.cgi

They specialize in providing genealogical and historical books for the family, local, and social historians.

Genealogical Publishing Company:
http://www.genealogical.com/

Genealogical Publishing Co., Inc. is the largest commercial publisher of genealogical reference books, textbooks, and how-to books in the world. Over the years, GPC and its subsidiaries, Clearfield Company and

Gateway Press, have published more than 5,000 titles in genealogy and related fields.

Genealogy Books:
http://www.genealogy-books.com/

GENEALOGY BOOKS was established in 1996. Currently, there are over 1,200 genealogy books listed here for sale which include books on immigration and passenger lists, probate records, county records (such as wills, deeds, marriages), obituaries, census, Bibles, civil war, revolutionary war, county histories, genealogies, family histories, family organizations, newsletters, Bible records, how-to-do-it manuals, research aids and textbooks from the United States, Canada, Germany, Great Britain, Ireland, Russia, Scotland and Wales, and many other genealogy books.

Genealogy Mall:
http://www.genealogymall.com/

The GenealogyMall™ is trying to become the hottest genealogy specialty address on the Internet— the one-stop place to go for all your family history needs. They will have something for everyone: professional genealogists, family researchers, as well as the hobbyist.

Government CD-ROMs:
http://www.access.gpo.gov/su_docs/sale/sale300.html

This site has a list of CD-ROM titles available through the Superintendent of Documents of the U.S. Government Printing Office (GPO). They sell CD-ROM titles published by a wide variety of federal government agencies, including the General Land Office Records CD.

Hearthstone Bookshop:
http://www.hearthstonebooks.com/

Their specialty is genealogy and related products. Just as your ancestors provisioned their wagons at a general store or trading post when journeying to new lands, they invite you to make their Web page a regular stop on your own "ancestral trail." They stock more titles from more publishers than any other genealogical dealer. They also carry software, CDs, charts, forms, and other items. Check out their listings at this site. They have a search engine that can search their whole database. They add new items monthly.

Iberian Publishing Company - Genealogy Books:
http://www.iberian.com/

This site contains Iberian Publishing Company's online genealogy catalog. They have supplied quality genealogical reference books for the Virginias and other Southeastern states since 1982.

Microfilm Catalogs:
http://gopher.nara.gov:70/1/genealog/holdings/catalogs/

National Archives Microfilm Publication indexes on the Internet.

Online Pioneers Genealogy Page:
http://www.eskimo.com/~mnarends/index.html

If you can't keep up with the escalating world of computers and genealogy, *Online Pioneers* newsletter is for you. A newsletter geared to new and experienced users alike, filled with informative, timely articles, *Online Pioneers* is a one-of-a-kind publication that covers both the online and offline computer genealogy community.

Willow Bend Books:
http://server.mediasoft.net/ScottC/

Willow Bend Books sells and publishes books, especially genealogical and historical materials. They represent themselves, Iberian Press, Family Line Publications, Heritage Books, Clearfield Company, Genealogical Publishing Company, Scholarly Resources, Masthoff Press, The Library of Virginia and some self-published authors.

Yates Publishing:
http://www.montana.com/yates/

Here you can search their online database "The Computerized Ancestor," visit their FTP site, or read their online catalog.

Ye Olde Genealogie Shoppe©:
http://www.yogs.com/

Pat and Ray Gooldy opened Ye Olde Genealogie Shoppe© in 1974, providing exhibits, lectures, classes, publications, and other genealogical services. They have numerous categories of special catalogs online for you to look at.

Zarahemla Book Shop - Genealogy Software:
http://www.zarahemla.com/gensoft.html

This site is a source for many genealogy software programs. It also includes a link to its LDS main bookshop.

Online Genealogy Publications

Digital Digest:
http://www.jb.com/~carla/

The Digital Digest is written by Carla & Dennis Ridenour. It is dedicated to the use of computers in the study of genealogy and family history. It contains online articles about genealogy and genealogy related computer subjects. The articles appear in their entirety, and can also be downloaded for offline reading.

Eastman's Online Genealogy Newsletter:
http://www.ancestry.com/home/eastarch.htm

This is a weekly summary by Richard Eastman of events and topics of interest to online genealogists.

The Family Tree Online:
http://www.teleport.com/~binder/famtree.shtml

They are an international genealogical publication which is in the process of bringing *The Family Tree Online* into the digital world. *The Family Tree*, in its hard copy version, is published bimonthly by the Ellen Payne Odom Genealogy Library in Moultrie, Georgia. As a repository for over ninety Scots Clans, the library serves as a central source of information and study to those with an interest in genealogy. In its sixth year, *The Family Tree* has all the latest news from numerous affiliations, and offers a refreshing perspective to celebrating our heritage.

The Global Gazette:
http://globalgenealogy.com/gazette.htm

The Global Gazette is Canada's bi-weekly Genealogy & Heritage Magazine.

The Hoosier Genealogist:
http://www.spcc.com/ihsw/thg.htm

This is the Web site of the online edition of the *The Hoosier Genealogist*. This quarterly publication, established by the Indiana Historical Society in 1961, is devoted to information on Hoosier family history. Some of the many primary research materials that may be contained in each issue include: Bible records, marriage records, estate records, school enumerations, probate and will records, land records, church records, naturalization records, pension records, alumni lists, items from old newspapers, obituaries, and old settlers' meetings.

Journal of Online Genealogy:
http://www.onlinegenealogy.com/

Welcome to the Journal of Online Genealogy. The Journal is a free electronic magazine which focuses on the use of online resources and techniques in genealogy and family history.

Online Databases for Genealogists

All-in-One Genealogy Search Page:
http://www.geocities.com/Heartland/Acres/8310/gensearcher.html

GenSearcher, the "All-in-One Genealogy Search Page" enables on-line genealogy research utilizing some of the best resources and sites on the Internet. This site is meant for convenience and utility–it is not meant to replace the referenced sites but merely to provide an extra door. Please visit the sites mentioned for more detailed search options, assistance, and access to a vast amount of genealogy information. This site has links to many of the best free genealogy databases online.

American Life Histories - WPA Project:
http://lcweb2.loc.gov/ammem/wpaquery.html

This Web site has a searchable database containing: American Life Histories: Manuscripts from the Federal Writers' Project, 1936-1940.

Ancestry Research Site:
http://www.ancestry.com/ancestry/search.asp

Their site contains the following: Social Security Death Index (SSDI) - the Death Master File; more than 51 million searchable records; Ancestry World Tree; and a 10-day free trial of many of their other databases.

Ancestry World Tree Search Site:
http://www.ancestry.com/home/ged/main.htm

The Web site of the Ancestry World Tree, a fully searchable database created by the contributions of fellow family history enthusiasts throughout the World. You can help the World Tree grow by contributing your own family tree (GEDCOM file).

Archives Web:
http://www.obd.nl/archivesweb.htm

This site contains links to national archives around the world, listed by country.

ArchivesUSA™ Home Page:
http://archives.chadwyck.com/

ArchivesUSA™ (available on CD-ROM or online by subscription—very expensive!) allows instant access to the special collection details of more than 4,400 repositories. It includes records, complete with detailed indexes, for approximately 100,000 individual collections. This is an exciting tool for finding manuscript sources that combines both NUCMC and NIDS in an easily searched format. Find out about it here. Look for it to use at large institutions with large budgets, or free at academic instituions.

Biography.com:
http://www.biography.com/find/index.html

Not strictly for genealogy, but the Biography.com database puts over 20,000 of the greatest lives, past and present, at your fingertips. Enter a name in their search box to discover who they were, what they did, and why.

BLM Land Patent Search Site:
http://www.glorecords.blm.gov/

Bureau of Land Management (BLM), Eastern States, General Land Office (GLO) Records Automation Web site. This site provides access to more than two million land records for the Eastern Public Land States (those 31 states bordering or east of the Mississippi). You have to sign up for the site, but it's free.

Books We Own Project:
http://www.rootsweb.com/~bwo/

Books We Own is a list of resources owned/accessed by ROOTS-L mailing list members and others who are willing to look up genealogical information and e-mail or snail mail it to others upon request. The available books are separated into categories. Some of these categories are: general information, surnames, various countries, the states listed by county, and more.

British Columbia Archives:
http://www.bcarchives.gov.bc.ca/index.htm

The British Columbia Archives is located in Victoria, British Columbia, Canada. It is the central archives service for the government of British Columbia, and provides research access to indexes of British Columbia marriage registrations for the years 1872 to 1921, and British Columbia death registrations for the years 1872 to 1976. Their "what's new" section highlights new additions and enhancements to this online service. Their online research library contains the North West Collection, with more than 10,000 publications catalogued. An extensive collection of newspapers on microfilm is provided by the Legislative Library of British Columbia.

California Heritage Digital Image Access Project:
http://sunsite.berkeley.edu/CalHeritage/

The California Heritage Collection is a "digital" archive containing photographs, pictures, and manuscripts from the collections of the Bancroft Library. It is an "archive" because it offers the public direct access to unique, primary source materials documenting California's rich history "in their original archival context." This is achieved by embedding digital representations of the primary sources directly within the documents—archival finding aids—created by the Bancroft Library's curators and archivists to describe the collections.

California State - USGenWeb Project:
http://www.compuology.com/cagenweb/

The California portion of The USGenWeb Project is set up to provide a single entry point for genealogical research in all counties in California. There are pages that list genealogical resources for each county. Also, a query page is available for every county in the state. Read and post genealogical queries there for free. Also available is the California USGenWeb Archives where collected databases are stored. In addition, these databases are indexed so you can find which files are available for any county in the state.

Cemetery Listing Association:
http://www.best.com/~gazissax/silence/altfunin.html

Search page for the Cemetery Listing Association (CLA). They were founded so that genealogists would be able to access cemetery records instantly and freely worldwide. The CLA database currently contains records from 90 cemeteries and 6830 graves.

Civil War Soldiers & Sailors System:
http://www.itd.nps.gov/cwss/

The Civil War Soldiers & Sailors System (CWSS) is a database containing basic facts about servicemen who served on both sides during the Civil War; a list of regiments in Union and Confederate Armies; identifications and descriptions of 384 significant battles of the war; references that identify the sources of the information in the database; and where to find more information. The CWSS is made possible by partnerships with the Federation of Genealogical Societies, the Genealogical Society of Utah, the United Daughters of the Confederacy, and others. More information about soldiers, sailors, regiments, and battles, and cemetery records will be added over time. The first phase contains more than 230,000 soldiers' names.

Clark County, Nevada Marriage Inquiry System:
http://www.co.clark.nv.us/RECORDER/MAR_DISC.HTM

Marriages are indexed on-line from 1984 through the present. For inquires about marriages prior to 1984 (from 1909 through 1983), you need to either visit their office to view the archived records, call, or mail them your request.

Confederate Pension Rolls, Veterans and Widows:
http://image.vtls.com/collections/CW.html

This collection consists of approved pension applications and amended applications filed by resident Virginia Confederate veterans and their widows. The applications contain statements pertaining to the service record of the applicants and may include medical evaluations, information about the income and property of the veterans or their widows, and, in the case of widows, the date and place of marriages.

Confederate Pensions - Texas State Archives:
http://link.tsl.state.tx.us/c/compt/pension.html

This site has a searchable index to the Confederate Pension claims held by the Texas State Archives.

Everton Publishers Site:
http://www.everton.com/index.html

This site gives you access to Everton's Genealogical Helper online. The Social Security Index database has more than 60 million records. You can also try a free trial of two of their subscription databases. They have many subscription databases. The subscription prices seem a little high: one month - $15.00, six months $29.50, one year $49.50.

Family Chronicle - Surname Origin List:
http://www.familychronicle.com/surname.htm

Where does that name begin? Actually, the origin of surnames varies greatly from place to place. Here are articles relevant to British surnames: first names, localities, occupations, nicknames, and even Chinese surnames.

Family Tree Maker's FamilyFinder Index:
http://www.familytreemaker.com/ffitop.html

The FamilyFinder Index has approximately 123 million names from census records, marriage records, social security death records, actual family trees, etc. About 20% of people who have ever lived in the United States are listed here; however, this site only shows which of their CD ROMs you need to buy to be able to view the data. This index contains **NO** actual genealogical data.

Funeral Net:
http://www.funeralnet.com/search.html

FuneralNet home page. They have more than 20,000 U.S. Funeral Homes listed. They claim that on their Web site you will find the most extensive funeral home directory on the Internet. The directory can lead you to funeral home Web sites in your area, as well as those around the country. If the funeral home you are looking for does not offer information online, their name, address, and phone number can often be found here.

GEN-WEB Site:
http://www.netins.net/showcase/pafways/genweb.htm

Gen-Web site with links to hundreds of GEDCOM files all over the world. The data is sorted by location, then by names.

GenConnect:
http://cgi.rootsweb.com/~genbbs/qindex.html

An automated query system for genealogists. Many of the county coordinators in the USGenWeb and WorldGenWeb Projects are using this system to bring you queries, biographies and obituaries for their counties. You definitely want to search and post queries in the counties or countries where your ancestors lived.

GENDEX:
http://www.gendex.com/

This link takes you to GENDEX, an enterprise devoted to advancing the progress of family history and genealogy research on the World Wide Web. This site indexes hundreds of World Wide Web databases containing genealogical data for more than two million individuals, and gives you the ability to locate and view data of interest to you on any of these databases – without having to go and visit each of the databases separately.

Genealogist's Index to the World Wide Web:
http://members.aol.com/genwebindx/index.htm

This index locates any name or surname you search for. It indexes the older USGenWeb queries as well as hundreds of GEDCOM files online. It now has some new features, including SOUNDEX searching, as well as searching by state and county. This site is maintained by John Rigdon.

Genealogy Databases @ Internets:
http://www.internets.com/sgeneal.htm

Genealogy Databases @ Internets contains links to many searchable databases, including: Canadian Genealogy Search Engine, Celtic Resources Scottish Irish Database, Federation of Genealogical Societies Index, Genealogy Library Database, Genealogy Resources on the Internet, GenWeb Database, Heritage Cascade, Illustrated International Glossary of Heraldry, Linkages Kinship Database, Mormon Databases,

Pence list of bulletin boards in genealogy, Pimbley's Dictionary of Heraldry, RAND Genealogy Club's Roots Surname List, Roots surname database, Silicon Valley PAF Program, surnames and surnames database.

Genealogy Exchange & Surname Registry:
http://www.aplusdata.com/genexchange/index.cfm

The Genealogy Exchange & Surname Registry is broken down into two sections, as the name indicates. In the Genealogy Exchange, you can find lots of genealogy resource information for both on and off line genealogy. The Surname Registry is divided into two parts. In the General Registry, you can post any surname you are researching. In Select Surname Registries, there are surname specific databases They plan to have more than fifty Select Surname Registries available on this site.

GenealogyLibrary.com:
http://www.GenealogyLibrary.com/

A new **FEE** subscription site featuring a rapidly-growing online collection of rare books, historical databases, and "family finding" resources. GenealogyLibrary.com was created by Brøderbund Software. They claim to put hundreds of rare, hard-to-find books right at your fingertips, 24 hours a day, and save you dozens of trips to distant libraries or weeks of waiting for inter-library loans. This Web site started on 1 June 1998, with more than 500 books and databases online. The cost is $39.99 for an annual subscription, or pay $5.99 per month for a monthly subscription.

GENSERV - Genealogical GEDCOM Server System:
http://www.genserv.com/

GENSERV is a large collection of genealogical data. They have more than 7.9 million names in 5,800+ GEDCOM databases online. They **CHARGE** for their services, but you get one search free. They have annual subscriptions ranging from $6.00 to $12.00.

Illinois Land Records:
gopher://gopher.uic.edu:70/11/library/libdb/landsale/

This archive contains transaction data for approximately 545,000 public domain land sales in Illinois, supplied by the Illinois Secretary of State and the State Archive to the University of Illinois at Chicago's University Library and Computer Center. The great majority of transactions date from the year 1815 to about 1880.

Index to Passenger Lists:
http://www.rootsweb.com/~ote/indexshp.htm

An index to many early American ship lists including: Definitions of Early Ships, Palatine Ships to Pennsylvania, Dutch & Huguenot Ships to New Netherland (New York), Ships to Nova Scotia, Miscellaneous Ships, Irish Ships to Boston, Ships to the Carolinas, Ships to New England & Connecticut, Huguenot Ships to Virginia, Ships to Virginia 1625-1626 & 1635, and an Index of all ships by year of sailing.

Kentucky Death Index 1911-1992:
gopher://ukcc.uky.edu:9105/2/

Will not work with Microsoft's Internet Explorer 4. This site has a searchable online database of Kentucky deaths from 1911 to 1992. Gives the date of death, age, place, volume number, certificate number and death volume number.

Kindred Konnections:
http://www.kindredkonnections.com/

Many of their services are free. It is their desire to provide you with valuable research tools at little or no cost. In the research interest area, you can both register your research interests, as well as search this database for others who may be working on similar lines. They have a wealth of genealogical books, tapes, and videos for purchase.

Lacy's Genealogy Gateway™ 5 to the Web:
http://www.polaris.net/~legend/gateway5.htm

They claim to be the largest online newspaper obituaries listing on the WWW. They have access to more than 140 Obituary Search links. The information you receive from each site varies.

Library of Virginia Archives and Manuscripts Database:
http://image.vtls.com:80/bible/virtua-basic.html

The Archives and Manuscript Database includes 8,700 catalog records for most materials received since the late 1980s. Several retrospective cataloging projects have been completed – most notably the cataloging of 4,700 family Bible records, and the records of the state Auditor of Public Accounts.

Lineages' Genealogy Site: Free Genealogy Queries:
http://www.lineages.com/queries/queries.asp

This is the free genealogy queries Web page on Lineages' Genealogy Site. Lineages has more than 29,000 genealogy queries online, some may have your ancestors' surnames. Let everyone know who your ancestors are with Lineages' free genealogy queries. It's an easy way to trace your family history.

Mayflower Passenger List:
http://members.aol.com/calebj/alphabet.html

A complete passenger list for the Mayflower. Based on the passenger list made by William Bradford in his journal, published under the title *Of Plymouth Plantation*, this list includes subsequent research in primary source records in England and America to fill in names Bradford did not give in full. Passengers are listed alphabetically by surname. Each head of household has a link which takes you to biographical and genealogical information about the passenger.

my-ged.com Server:
http://www.my-ged.com/db/sites

This site is a free GEDCOM server. This is a site where people can share their genealogy with others.

National Archives and Records Administration (NAIL):
http://www.nara.gov/nara/nail/nailgen.html

NARA Archival Information Locator (NAIL). Currently, the searchable NAIL database contains only limited genealogical data, including descriptions of 52,000 case files of Cherokee, Creek, and Seminole applications for enrollment to the Five Civilized Tribes (Dawes Commission) between 1898 and 1914, and descriptions of 50,000 Fort Smith, Arkansas criminal case files. Files are updated weekly.

National Archives Records Administration (NARA):
http://www.nara.gov/

Home page for the National Archives and Records Administration (NARA). NARA is the government agency responsible for overseeing the management of the records of the federal government. NARA ensures for the citizen, the public servant, the President, Congress, and the Courts ready access to essential evidence that documents the rights of American citizens, the actions of federal officials, and the national experience.

Obituary Daily Times Web Site:
http://www.best.com/~shuntsbe/obituary/

This new free genealogical tool for family researchers is growing fast. They are receiving obituaries from almost every state and province in the US and Canada, and some international. If you are searching for descendants of a particular family group, this is the exchange group you want (i.e. all of ONESURNAME family).

OLIVE TREE Genealogy Homepage:
http://www.rootsweb.com/~ote/

This is an interesting genealogy page created by Lorine McGinnis Schulze. She has tried to incorporate a little bit of everything – surnames she's searching, Dutch naming patterns of the 1600s to assist you in finding those elusive ancestors, passenger lists from ships sailing to the New World, Militia muster rolls, source materials for different locations and eras, and other items of interest.

Online Bible Records:
http://www.genealogy-books.com/idxbible.htm

Every week they try to add some Bible records for your viewing. The Bibles are US-wide and some of them very old. Be sure and bookmark this page and check back regularly.

On-line Books:
http://alabanza.com/kabacoff/Inter-Links/library/books.html

This Web page contains pointers to full-text books available on-line.

Online Genealogical Database Index:
http://www.gentree.com/gentree2.html

The Genealogical Database Index contains links to all known genealogical databases searchable through the Web. It is limited to searchable databases and does **NOT** include links to sites that are devoted to a family, unless they have a searchable database.

Online Catalog Virtua-Web: Word/Phrase Search:
http://image.vtls.com/bible/virtua-basic.html

This site provides an archives and manuscripts database search. The database also includes Bible records.

PERiodical Source Index (PERSI):
http://www.ancestry.com/PERSI.htm

PERSI is a comprehensive subject index, produced by the Allen County Public Library, to genealogy and local history periodicals written in English and also French-Canadian since 1800. The collection also includes literature dating from the 1700s (the collection before 1800 is less complete). PERSI online represents some 27 volumes in print. PERSI is available at this Ancestry Web site for a reasonable monthly **FEE**, or by purchase on CD ROM from Ancestry, Inc.

Repositories of Primary Sources:
http://www.uidaho.edu/special-collections/Other.Repositories.html

This site has a listing of over 2,700 Web sites describing holdings of manuscripts, archives, rare books, historical photographs, and other primary sources for the research scholar. All links have been tested for correctness and appropriateness.

RSL (Roots Surname List):
http://www.rootsweb.com/rootsweb/searches/rslsearch.html

This site lets you perform an Interactive search of the current Roots Surname List messages. These surnames are submitted by about 34,691 genealogists. You must enter at least the first two letters of the surname (that is, at least "sm" for Smith or "is" for Isaacson). This is an effective way to find others researching your surnames in your areas of interest.

Roots-L Web Page:
http://www.rootsweb.com/roots-l/

ROOTS-L is a mailing list for people who are interested in genealogy. It's not the only one. There are many other genealogical mailing lists. ROOTS-L is currently the oldest and largest genealogical mailing list. They had more than 8,000 subscribers in early 1997.

RootsWeb Genealogical Data Cooperative:
http://www.rootsweb.com/

RootsWeb is really about search engines – databases and software married together to let you search for records online. You'll find they already have enhanced search engines for the 232,474-name Roots Surname List and the Roots Location List. As resources allow, they will bring more databases (like the Social Security Death Index, census extracts, and county history indices) online.

RootsWeb has online search engines located at:
http://www.rootsweb.com/rootsweb/searches/

This site allows you to search: the 207,972 name Roots Surname List (RSL); the Roots Location List (RLL); Arkansas databases; California databases; Louisiana databases; South Carolina databases; South Dakota databases; Tennessee databases; Vermont databases; Wisconsin databases; search Usenet newsgroups; and search the ROOTS-L archives.

Rootsweb Mailing List Archives:
http://searches.rootsweb.com/~archiver/

An area on Rootsweb that contains archives for many genealogy mail lists. You can view old messages to those mail lists.

Scott McGee's GenWeb Page:
http://genealogy.org/~smcgee/genweb/genweb.html

See the *Royal92* file (which has Europe's royalty), *Mayflo9* file (the latest update of the Mayflower database which already had 10 generations of descendants and 25 of ancestors of the Mayflower passengers), *Pool* file (which has many medieval genealogies and a "descent from Adam" ancestry based on biblical references), and the *Murphy* file (which has been recently updated and now has more than 26,000 entries).

Social Security Death Index:
http://www.ancestry.com/ancestry/search.asp

This site allows you to search the complete Social Security Death Index online. (March 1997 edition)

Tombstone Transcription Project:
http://www.rootsweb.com/~cemetery/

This is a new project to create a database of tombstone inscriptions. They feel we need to record tombstone inscriptions now – before they are lost forever to the winds and the rains. Though many cemeteries have already been recorded by various genealogical societies, just as many have not. And of those recorded, how accessible is that data to the world? If we join together and do this recording, we will guarantee that our ancestors are not forgotten.

Traveller Southern Families:
http://genealogy.traveller.com/genealogy/

The Traveller Southern Families site is dedicated to genealogy, the science or study of family descent. Being Southern born and Southern bred, they have concentrated on Southern families and related Web sites. At their site, you will find family trees donated by folks like you (The Cousin Finder), a Web bulletin board service which allows anyone to post genealogical inquires (WebBoard), and Internet references to hundreds of other excellent Web sites containing invaluable genealogical information.

US Biographies Project:
http://www.starbase21.com/kybiog/usbiog.html

The US Biographies Project was organized by Jeff Murphy in May of 1997. The project used the established KY Biographies Project as a model. State coordinators were sought to set up their own state project. They were offered the system design and tools created for the KY project, but were free to set up their project in any way they chose.

USGenWeb Archives:
http://www.rootsweb.com/~usgenweb/

The USGenWeb Archives was developed to present actual transcriptions of public domain records on the Internet. This huge undertaking is the cooperative effort of volunteers who either have electronically formatted files (census records, marriage bonds, wills, and other public documents) or are willing to transcribe this information to contribute. An index is set up for every state.

USGenWeb Archives Search Engine:
http://searches.rootsweb.com/usgwarch.html

This search engine can search all of the files in the USGenWeb Archives for any state in the US.

USGenWeb Federal Census Project State Index:
http://www.usgenweb.org/census/

The USGenWeb Census Project was established to transcribe Federal and State Census Records and the posting of that information on the Internet. The actual transcribed census records will be placed in the USGenWeb Archives.

The USGenWeb Project:
http://www.usgenweb.org/

This project is an effort to organize the genealogy information and materials on the Internet. It is supported by thousands of volunteers across the country. Basically, the system is organized by states and counties. Each county has a coordinator responsible for maintaining a site listing resources available for that county. You'll also find files of genealogy records organized by state and county. The USGenWeb project page has links to all of the State USGenWeb pages, where information is set up for every county in every state. This is a great place to start your research and you'll come back to it time and time again.

Veteran and Military Web Sites:
http://members.aol.com/veterans/warlib6.htm

This site contains numerous hot links to various veteran and military Web sites.

WDC GenWeb Project Home Page:
http://www.primenet.com/~dlytton/wdc/

The World Descendant Charts Genealogy Web Project was originally conceived as a home for those who do not have their own Web pages to put their genealogy on display. (Even if you do have your own Web page, you are invited to participate). WDC is a noncommercial, nonprofit project.

Webified Genealogy Home Page:
http://www.surfutah.com/web/webgene/index.html

Webified Genealogy (WebGene) is a tool produced by Rex Myer to view GEDCOM files on the Web. It can dynamically produce graphical pedigree charts, descendant charts, and outlines of genealogy information from a GEDCOM file. Keep in mind that "dynamically produce them" means that you don't have to have a bunch of pages and directories which contain the Web pages of your genealogy. All you need is the GEDCOM file (and the tool). Also it is best viewed with Netscape, but other browsers can see it too.

World Genealogy Web Project Headquarters:
http://www.worldgenweb.org/

This site is an effort to organize world wide genealogy materials on the Internet. It is supported by many volunteers all around the world. The system is organized by countries. Each country has a coordinator responsible for maintaining a site of resources which are available for that country. The World GenWeb Project is an outgrowth of The USGenWeb Project.

Genealogy Tools & Training

Ancestors - The New Genealogy Series:
http://www2.kbyu.org/ancestors/

KBYU-TV, in association with the Public Broadcasting Service, is pleased to present the home page for *Ancestors*, a family history and genealogy series that aired on PBS stations. Whether you're new to genealogy, or an expert in past generations, this is a place you do not want to miss.

Ask Quailind:
http://www.AskQuailind.com/

This is a link to a paid (**fee**) service. They have an information and document delivery service for genealogists and family historians. They will search records in the Sutro Library holdings, or from the microfilm publications of the National Archives - Pacific Region (SF), for a small fee.

Birth Year Calculator:
http://home.mem.net/~rac7253/gen/cenindx.htm

This site will calculate a persons birth year based on their age on the census information. You simply click on the year of the census and it will give you a table of ages and birth years.

Calendar Creator:
http://www.stud.unit.no/USERBIN/steffent/kalender.pl

The Calendar Creator can create a calendar for any year you wish. It will accept any year between 0001 and 4000. If you write a year between 1 and 99, the calendar thinks you mean 1901-1999, so if you really want to see the year 25 AD, you will have to type "025," which will give you the year 25 AD. Just input the year and a calendar will be created for that year.

Carl Sandburg College Genealogy Classes:
http://www.asc.csc.cc.il.us/~mneill/csc/index.html

Genealogy on the Internet sponsored by Carl Sandburg College, Galesburg, Illinois. They offer online courses such as Genealogy on the Internet, Beginning Genealogy, and Intermediate Genealogy.

Census - Lookups:
http://wymple.gs.net/~longstrt/census.html

This site is a meeting place, where researchers and volunteers can meet who are willing to look up information in copies which they may have of the Federal Census. This Web site was begun on the 8th of May, 1998, and hopefully will eventually include every county in the U.S.

Center for Life Stories Preservation:
http://www.storypreservation.com/

The Center for Life Stories Preservation is a resource dedicated to helping people capture their family and life stories. Their mission is to educate people about the power of life stories, empower them to celebrate and preserve their stories before they're lost, and support them in accomplishing that goal through a variety of methods.

County Finder:
http://www.mit.edu:8001/geo/

This is an excellent aid for all genealogists. You can find the county name for any city in the entire United States at this site. This is very convenient.

Family Photo Historian:
http://www.geocities.com/Heartland/2878/indexnf.html

This Web page was set up to help educate people in the methods of finding, organizing, restoring, and preserving valuable family photos.

Federal Census Indexes Online:
http://www.nara.gov/publications/microfilm/census/census.html

This site contains the 1790-1890 Federal Population Census index catalogs from the National Archives. You can look up the roll numbers for the census before you head off to the archives.

Frequently Occurring Names from the 1990 Census:
http://www.census.gov/ftp/pub/genealogy/www/freqnames.html

This site contains frequently occurring first names and surnames from the 1990 census. These files contain only the frequency with which the name appears in the census, not specific individual information.

Genealogy:
http://execpc.com/~dboals/geneo.html

Part of the History/Social Studies Web Site for K-12 teachers, this site contains more than a hundred links to other great Web sites (including some great "how to" sites).

Genealogy Articles & Files:
http://www.qal.berkeley.edu/~suggs/history/genealogy/

The genealogical information on this Web page is divided into the following categories: (1) family histories, charts, and records; (2) other genealogies; (3) classes and articles; (4) miscellaneous downloads.

Genealogy Helplist United States:
http://posom.com/hl/

The Genealogy Helplist consists of volunteers who are willing to help others with specific items at institutions near them, or help with other information easily accessible to them. Help is available all across the United States.

Genealogy Launch Pad:
http://http.tamu.edu:8000/~mbg5500/genealogy/gen_page.html

This page provides summary documentation about the resources available at the LDS Family History Library. It has important links to genealogy resources on the Internet. It also provides a one-stop resource for those wanting to know how to begin genealogical research.

Genealogy Resource Page:
http://www.pacificnet.net/~reunions/

The Genealogy Resource Page provides family history "how to" information in the following areas: U.S. Census; Social Security Death Index; California Indexes - Marriage, Divorce, and Death; North Carolina - Marriage Bond Abstracts 1741 - 1868; links to other useful genealogy sites on the Web.

Genealogy's Most Wanted:
http://www.citynet.net/mostwanted/

On these pages you will find the surnames and known information on a person that is "MOST WANTED." The information listed has been submitted by a researcher who is requesting your help. The researcher's e-mail address or their snail mail address has been provided should you have any information or leads to assist them in their search for their "MOST WANTED."

ICONnect:
http://www.ala.org/ICONN/

ICONnect Internet training page. School library media specialists, teachers, and students will find the opportunity to learn the skills necessary to navigate the information superhighway right here. It contains online Internet training courses.

LDS Church - Family History Information:
http://www.lds.org/Family_History/How_Do_I_Begin.html

This is an official site of the LDS church. It gives the five basic steps to get started in discovering your family history. Discover the records and services available at your Family History Center™. Locate the Family History Center™ closest to you.

Lineages Genealogy Queries Page:
http://www.lineages.com/queries/BrowseByCountry.asp

Lineages' free genealogy queries are a good way to help you locate others with a common family history.

NARA's "The Genealogy Page":
http://www.nara.gov/genealogy/

This site provides many of the finding aids, guides, and research tools that can prepare the genealogist for a visit to one of the National Archives and Records Administration (NARA) facilities.

NetGuide - Genealogists Guide to the Internet:
http://emcee.com/NGS/netguide/

Written by George Archer. This guide is a work in progress. The Net is constantly changing, and this guide reflects these changes. Not everything described there will work well or all the time because sites close and files and addresses change. **Warning:** If downloaded and printed out, it may be over 12,000 pages.

New Jerusalem Home Page:
http://www.new-jerusalem.com/genealogy/genealogy.html

This site has a list of genealogy resources. It also has "The Genealogy Lady." She takes your questions about genealogy and answers them.

NGS "Suggestions for Beginners":
http://www.genealogy.org/~ngs/sugbeg.html

The (U.S.) National Genealogical Society's instructions on how to get started in family history research.

NGS "Standards for Sound Genealogical Research":
http://www.genealogy.org/~ngs/standsgr.html
"Standards for Using Records Repositories and Libraries":
http://www.genealogy.org/~ngs/standrrl.html

The (U.S.) National Genealogical Society has released these two standards for genealogical researchers. The society hopes that these will be broadly disseminated and taken to heart by genealogists, especially new researchers. Anyone interested in researching their ancestry should read these documents and consider them carefully.

Nicknames and Naming Traditions:
http://www.tngenweb.usit.com/franklin/frannick.htm

A knowledge of the various nicknames can help us better identify our ancestors. This site does not include some of the more obvious names. Remember, there can be an Eliza and an Elizabeth in the same family. Also, it is not uncommon to find two children with the same name.

NUCMC Catalog:
http://lcweb.loc.gov/coll/nucmc/nucmccat.html

National Union Catalog of Manuscript Collections (NUCMC) contains descriptions of approximately 72,300 collections located in 1406 different repositories with approximately 1,085,000 index references to topical subjects and personal, family, corporate, and geographic names. Cataloging for the volumes from 1986/87 to 1993 is available in the RLIN AMC file, but the cataloging in the earlier volumes is not currently available in machine readable form. Limited searches for manuscript sources may be made here. See Archives USA™ for a more complete (but hard to find) search tool.

Occupations Descriptions:
http://www.onthenet.com.au/~tonylang/occupa.htm

In your research, when stuck with the question of what the occupation listed on the certificate or census film meant, you can come to this Web page. It contains a list of occupations that can be invaluable in understanding our ancestors day to day living.

Old Disease Names & Their Modern Definitions:
http://www.netusa1.net/~hartmont/medicalterms.htm

This Web site gives a very good listing of old diseases along with their modern names.

OneLook Dictionaries:
http://www.onelook.com/

The OneLook Dictionaries site is a great place to look up those words you don't understand or aren't familiar with. It allows you to search for a word in 183 dictionaries/glossaries on the Internet at one time. It can find legal terms and Internet terms with ease.

Origins of Family Names:
http://www.rootscomputing.com/howto/names/names.htm

This Web page is by Ron Collins. A surname is a name added to a baptismal or given name for the purposes of making it more specific, and of indicating family relationship or descent. Classified according to origin, most surnames fall into four general groups: (1) those formed from the given name of the sire; (2) those arising from bodily or personal characteristics; (3) those derived from locality or place of residence; and (4) those derived from occupation.

Our Ancestors Nicknames:
http://www.uftree.com/UFT/HowTos/SettingOut/nickname1.html

This Web site gives many common nicknames and various spellings for names. Name changes and spelling variants give novice and professional researchers a headache.

Repeat Performance:
http://www.repeatperformance.com/

They have audio recordings of genealogical seminars and conferences for sale. They can be used as an educational tool for genealogists or people searching for family tree, ancestry, lineage, or adoption records. These tapes may be useful in your research and education.

Research Tools - CD Lookups:
http://www.seidata.com/~lhoffman/cdlist.html

This site has a list of persons who are willing to do limited look ups from CD-ROM's for free. They have numerous CD-ROM titles available for searching.

Institute of Genealogy & Historical Research:
http://www.samford.edu/schools/ighr/ighr.html

The Samford Institute of Genealogy and Historical Research offers a week of intensive genealogical study led by nationally prominent genealogical educators. A student may choose one of seven courses ranging from a course for beginners to courses for specialized topics. The Institute is academically and professionally oriented and is cosponsored by the Board for Certification of Genealogists.

Soundex Conversion Tool:
http://searches.rootsweb.com/cgi-bin/Genea/soundex.sh

This is a searchable index by the Rand Genealogy Club. The Soundex system is the means established by the National Archives to index the

U.S. censuses (beginning with 1880). It codes together surnames of the same and similar sounds but of variant spellings. Soundexes are arranged by state, Soundex code of the surname, and then given name.

Spectrum Virtual University:
http://www.vu.org/

Spectrum is an online university dedicated in the belief that knowledge is the bridge to freedom, prosperity, and hope on planet Earth. Their virtual campus on the World Wide Web is the largest online learning community on the Internet and more than some half-million people from 128 countries have attended their online classes.

Surnames: What's in a Name? Origins & Meanings:
http://clanhuston.com/name/surnames.htm

This site is by Broken Arrow Publishing. What did your medieval ancestors do? Or where did they live? Surnames – our last names – tell a story that has been handed down for hundreds of years, and yet many people don't know what the story means. Most last names have a unique history that tells us about the medieval ancestors who gave us our surnames. What is the meaning of your name? If you don't know, take heart – most queries are easily answered.

Surname Registry - Horus:
http://www.ucr.edu/h-gig/surdata/nameform.html

This site contains the H-GIG Genealogical Registry for registry of surnames. It was set up by the University of California, Riverside.

SurnameWeb:
http://www.surnameweb.org/

This is the Web site of the Surname Genealogy Web Project. This page links to surnames from every country in the world. It contains the surname registry, surname resource centers, other surname resources and databases, and the SurnameRing.

The Genealogy Anonymous FTP site:
ftp://ftp.cac.psu.edu/pub/genealogy/INDEX.html

This site contains programs and text files related to genealogy. Many of the programs and files in this index have simple descriptions after the file names. Many descriptions include a link to a home, another Web page with newer versions, or more information about the program or file. You can download any of these programs from here.

Tracing Mormon Pioneers:
http://www.vii.com/~nelsonb/pioneer.htm

The purpose of this Web page is to provide tips for those tracing their Mormon Pioneers' ancestry from Europe and South Africa to Salt Lake City, Utah. It is the 150th year since the arrival of the first pioneer company to Salt Lake City in 1847, and many descendants of these pioneers have not traced their pioneer heritage. This page will assist those descendants in their quest.

Treasure Maps:
http://www.firstct.com/fv/tmapmenu.html

The how-to do genealogy Web site. Five steps to getting started on your family history. How-to get past the "Stone Wall Syndrome." A fascinating tutorial on "Deciphering Old Handwriting," from a course taught by Sabina J. Murray, and many more training aids and links.

Twenty Ways to Avoid Genealogical Grief:
http://www.smartlink.com/~leverich/20ways.html

Here are some suggestions for beginners to prevent misfortune when learning how to do genealogical research. Many of these tips are "old-hat" to experienced genealogists, but it's always good to remind ourselves of the basics of research.

US Land & Property Research Training Course:
http://users.arn.net/~billco/uslpr.htm

This course, offered by the International Internet Genealogical Society University, is a self-paced set of lessons on the basics of land and property research in the United States. This type of research is often daunting and somewhat intimidating to genealogists, especially those just beginning to encounter land grants, deeds, and other forms of property acquisition and transfer.

Vital Records Information:
http://www.inlink.com/~nomi/vitalrec/index.html

This page contains information about where to obtain vital records from each state, territory and county of the United States. The information on these pages is constantly being updated with information obtained from other genealogists. If you find any mistakes in the information provided, please let them know so they can make updates. If you obtain any new information about the prices of vital records, please e-mail them that information also

Where to Write for Vital Records (FTM):
http://www.familytreemaker.com/statelst.html

Family Tree Maker's site gives information on where to write for records sorted by state.

Citing Sources & Writing Skills

Citing Online Sources:
http://www.nhmccd.cc.tx.us/groups/lrc/kc/mla-internet.html

Kingwood College Library site contains specific examples of citing online sources and the general rules for citing electronic sources.

Guide to Grammar and Spelling:
http://www.well.com/user/mmcadams/copy.editing.html

An online copy-editing tutorial. An introduction to the procedures of copy editing for consumer, trade, and specialty magazines.

My Virtual Reference Desk - Grammar, Usage and Style:
http://www.refdesk.com/factgram.html

A Web page set up by Bob Drudge. This page contains information on grammar, usage, and style.

Online English Grammar Help:
http://www.edunet.com/english/grammar/index.html

This grammar help has been put online by Anthony Hughes.

Online Resources for Writers:
http://webster.commnet.edu/writing/writing.htm

A list of Internet writing sites.

Copyright Information

The Big C: Information about Copyrights:
http://www.tomkidding.com/musicbiz/thebigc/

Information on this Web page is intended only as a guide. Information supplied here has been compiled from literature received from the Copyright Office in Washington DC. They have tried to explain the various types of copyright forms.

Copyright Myths:
http://www.clari.net/brad/copymyths.html

Ten Big Myths about copyright explained. An attempt to answer some of the common myths about copyright seen on the net, and cover issues related to copyright and USENET/Internet publication.

Family Tree Maker, Who Owns Genealogy?:
http://www.familytreemaker.com/14_cpyrt.html

An article written by Gary B. Hoffman discussing: "Who owns a compiled genealogy? The one who compiled it? The one who possesses a copy? The one whose ancestors are the subject of the compilation? Anyone? No one"?

Government Site: Copyright Basics:
ftp://ftp.loc.gov/pub/copyright/circs/circ01.html

This U.S. government site includes details on all copyright laws.

USGenWeb's FAQs about Copyright:
http://www.usroots.com/faqs/uscopyrt.htm

This site is maintained by The USGenWeb Project. They feel it is vital for genealogists and family historians to understand copyright laws, not only for the protection of others' rights, but to ensure that they retain the rights to their own work. This covers many aspects of copyright law, including many links to other copyright sites.

Mail Lists, Newsgroups, & Chat Sites

AGI - Chat Room:
http://agi.hypermart.net/chat2.htm

The Internet Genealogical Directory's free Chat Room Web page. They also have a French speaking Chat Room online, located at **http://agi.hypermart.net/chat1.htm**

Genealogy Related Newsgroups:
http://www.meertech.demon.co.uk/genuki/newsgrou.htm

This site contains a list of genealogy related newsgroups which are formed by the soc.genealogy.* hierarchy. It contains descriptions of the various newsgroups of genealogical interest. It also lists where the newsgroup messages are archived, if they are. Also mentioned are any associated mail lists. This particular page is updated on the 8th of every month.

GenForum:
http://www.genforum.com/

GenForum is a conglomeration of message boards (some people call them queries, they call them forums). Anyone can post a message to these forums and immediately have their data shared with other researchers. From their main page, you can access our over 8,200 forums devoted to specific surnames, states, countries, and general topics. They also have a genealogy chat section. You may find their Web site both fun and useful.

GMW Chat Page:
http://www.citynet.net/mostwanted/prechat.htm

The Genealogy's Most Wanted Chat Page is for the online discussion of genealogy. When the chat page is operating, several regulars frequent it. Should you wish to join with them and ask genealogy questions, just simply pick a handle (nickname) and join in.

List Servers, Newsgroups and Special Home Pages:
http://www.eskimo.com/~chance/

Contains a listing of mail lists that may be of value to genealogists. If there is a newsgroup associated with the mail list, then that is indicated also. The site also contains links to special genealogy home pages.

Mail Lists:
http://users.aol.com/johnf14246/gen_mail.html

This is a very complete list of genealogy mail lists by John Fuller. Mail lists contained on his Web page are divided in five categories: General, Geographic/Non-USA, Geographic/USA, Software, and Surnames.

Newsgroups on the Internet:
http://members.aol.com/johnf14246/gen_use.html

This is a list of genealogy related newsgroups on the Internet. This site is maintained by John Fuller.

The DALnet Genealogy Channels:
http://www.geocities.com/SiliconValley/1641/genechat.html

J. Peter Haliburton (PeterH) and J. Ron Grassi (ColSandrs) are the founders of the genealogy channels on DALnet. If you are not familiar with IRC (Internet Relay Chat), you are really missing out on one of the most lively spots on the Internet. The genealogy chat groups are #Genealogy and #Genealogy2.

Virus Hoaxes:
http://www.symantec.com/avcenter/hoax.html

Many times in e-mail lists and newsgroups messages are passed about viruses. Although there are thousands of viruses discovered each year, there are still some that only exist in the imaginations of the public and the press. This is Web site contains a comprehensive list of viruses that DO NOT EXIST, despite rumor of their creation and distribution.

Locating Living People

411 Directories:
http://www.four11.com/

The White Pages of the Internet. You can search for phone numbers or e-mail addresses at this site.

555-1212.com:
http://www.555-1212.com/

On-line business and personal directories. Includes area code look-up; e-mail addresses, telephone numbers, and a Web site directory.

American Directory Assistance:
http://www.lookupusa.com/lookupusa/ada/ada.htm

This service lets you look up businesses or people by name, anywhere in the United States, and get their addresses and phone numbers. If you know the city, your search will be faster. If not, you can search by state. This search also works for many people who have **UNLISTED** numbers.

Bigfoot:
http://www.bigfoot.com/

Bigfoot claims to have the Internet's largest collection of e-mail addresses and "white page" listings. You can use it to find your family, friends, and colleagues.

Internet Address Finder:
http://www.iaf.net/

Internet Address Finder (IAF) is the easiest and most comprehensive e-mail White Pages on the Internet. Search for user by name. Wildcards ("*") are allowed in their searches.

Online Telephone Directories:
http://phonebooks.home.ml.org/

This site provides links to a very complete list of online telephone directories from all over the world.

People Search USA:
http://www.infospaceinc.com/people.html

Find more than 112 million listings of people and businesses. You can also search for e-mail addresses. This site also has a search index for people in Canada.

Reverse Area Code Directory:
http://in-132.infospace.com/_1_260770243__info/npa/npa.html

Did you ever get a phone number and wonder what part of the US it was in? You can search this directory for area codes in the United States, Canada, and the Caribbean. Find the city, state, and time zone.

Reverse Look Up Directory:
http://in-132.infospace.com/_1_260770243__info/reverse.htm

Did you ever have an address or phone number and wonder who it belonged to? You can search this directory for area codes, addresses or phone numbers in the United States, Canada, and the Caribbean.

Search International, Inc.:
http://www.searchint.com/

Search International, Inc. is exclusively in the missing persons business, with their primary focus being the location of missing heirs and beneficiaries. They also have a National Adoption Registry, Inc. where adoptees and birth parents are reunited.

The Seeker Magazine:
http://www.the-seeker.com/mainpage.htm

This site is dedicated to helping you find your missing friends or relatives. If you are looking for someone, this site has many ways to help you accomplish the task.

Switchboard - Searchable Telephone Directory:
http://www.switchboard.com/

A free searchable database to find friends, colleagues, and old roommates.

WhoWhere?:
http://www.whowhere.com/

This site allows you to search for a person's e-mail address on the Internet.

Zip Code Information:
http://www.usps.gov/ncsc/

This site has the U.S. Postal Service Address and Zip Code Information database. You can lookup new 9 digit zip codes here.

Other Computer Software Sites

DeLorme On-line Store:
http://www.delorme.com/

This is the home page for DeLorme, the makers of Street Atlas USA, the AAA Map'n'Go program, and the DeLorme Tripmate GPS Receiver.

E-TTACHMENT:
http://www.dataviz.com/Products/ETO/ETO_Home.html

Sometimes when you open an e-mail message and find garbage text at the end of the message, looking as if a monkey had typed it, and no attached files. At other times you are able to save the attached file, but Windows is unable to open it. This commercial program solves these e-mail attachment problems. This software is for Windows 95 only.

McAfee (Anti-virus):
http://www.mcafee.com/prod/av/av.asp

Many companies worldwide depend on McAfee for system-wide anti-virus solutions. With a 68% worldwide market share and anti-virus products for DOS, Windows, Macintosh, Unix and OS/2, McAfee is a leader in computer virus detection.

NewsRover:
http://www.newsrover.com/

News Rover is the ultimate tool for extracting information from Usenet newsgroups. News Rover automates the process of searching for messages containing keywords and phrases you are interested in. It downloads them and allows you to view just those messages that match your interests, with the keywords highlighted for easy reading. NewsRover does all of this automatically while you are at work, sleeping, or browsing the net. NewsRover does the work, so you don't have to waste time hunting for messages about your surnames and topics of interest on Usenet newsgroups.

Norton Anti Virus:
http://www.symantec.com/avcenter/

The Norton Anti-Virus trial version is now available online. Norton is another of the giants in the field of computer virus detection.

Oil Change:
http://www.cybermedia.com/products/oilchange/ochome.html

This program updates software on your computer automatically. Some of the problems on your PC have an easy solution in the form of software updates and bug fixes. Oil Change seeks out these updates from the Internet and automatically installs them on your computer.

Quarterdeck Corporation:
http://www.quarterdeck.com/

Quarterdeck Corporation publishes WebCompass, Procomm Plus, CleanSweep, HiJaak, and many other computer software programs genealogists may find generally useful.

Shareware.com:
http://www.shareware.com/

Many general shareware and freeware programs are available for downloading. Contains programs for most operating systems.

SupportHelp.com:
http://www.supporthelp.com/

SupportHelp.com is your one-stop-shop for locating technical support contact information from many of the hardware and software manufacturers. Technical support telephone numbers, e-mail addresses, and direct Web-site hot links are only a swift click away. Check this site for help with hardware or software problems.

Tucows:
http://tucows.abac.com/tucows/

One of the world's best collections of Internet software, TUCOWS is the place on the Web to access the latest and greatest Windows 95/98, Windows 3.1, and Macintosh Internet software. All software available at this site is performance rated and checked for viruses.

Virus Hoax Site:
http://ciac.llnl.gov/ciac/CIACHoaxes.html

Sometimes the computer virus you read about on the Internet isn't really a virus. So, before you panic and give away your computer for fear of the latest computer virus rumors, check this site. It contains explanations of many of the virus hoaxes you hear about on the Net.

Whew!:
http://www.wordcruncher.com/whew.html

This program indexes your e-mail messages. Whew! offers a fast powerful solution for finding specific e-mail messages. WordCruncher searches save time and effort by showing all of the search results at once, and by showing the search words in context.

Internet Search Tools

All-in-One Genealogy Search Page:
http://www.geocities.com/Heartland/Acres/8310/gensearcher.html

GenSearcher, the "All-in-One Genealogy Search Page" enables on-line genealogy research utilizing some of the best resources and sites on the Internet. This site is meant for convenience and utility–it is not meant to replace the referenced sites but merely to provide an extra door. Please visit the sites mentioned for more detailed search options, assistance, and access to a vast amount of genealogy information. This site has links to many of the best free genealogy databases online.

Alta Vista:
http://altavista.digital.com/

Alta Vista gives you access to one of the largest Web indexes containing 31 million Web pages located on 627,000 servers (1,158,000 host names), and four million articles from 14,000 Usenet newsgroups. Alta Vista is consulted more than 31 million times per weekday. It has excellent summaries and finds some stuff (like obituaries) that other search engines haven't indexed yet. Also, Alta Vista has added a second Usenet newsgroup search feature.

EuroSeek:
http://www.euroseek.net/

A search engine set up to let you search in many different areas of the world. In addition, it lets you search in many different languages.

Excite:
http://www.excite.com/

With Excite you can search the entire Web, NewsTracker, Excite Web Reviews, or Usenet newsgroups.

Family Tree Maker's Internet FamilyFinder:
http://www.familytreemaker.com/ifftop.html

Family Tree Maker's Internet FamilyFinder is a revolutionary new approach to finding your ancestors on the Internet. It is designed to be a single, comprehensive search tool for locating names in all of the genealogy data on the World Wide Web. They have specialized in searching and indexing genealogical Web sites. They index the entire site, not just the first paragraphs as most of the other search engines do.

Filez - Search FTP Sites:
http://www.filez.com/

This site can search through more than 75 million files on thousands of FTP servers for freeware, shareware, and commercial software to download.

Findspot:
http://www.findspot.com/

This site has links to numerous search tools. It also gives tips on using some of the more popular search engines.

HotBot:
http://www.hotbot.com/

One of the newer and easier Web-wide search engines of all those we have seen to date. HotBot makes it very easy to perform advanced queries. All you do is point-and-click to choose the advanced options. Also, the 50 million Web pages it indexes are an awesome number to be searched from one location.

I Found It! Genealogy Search Engine:
http://www.gensource.com/ifoundit/index.htm

I Found It! is a directory of genealogy related sites on the world wide web. Your search criteria are compared to information about the site provided by the owner. You'll find this site most useful by searching for a surname instead of full names, or a ship name instead of a passenger. One major benefit to this directory is that only genealogy sites are permitted to be indexed.

Infoseek:
http://www.infoseek.com/

In the February, 1997 issue of *PC Computing*, Infoseek gets the highest rating (five-stars) and this praise: "Aimless Web wandering is fine, but if you're on a mission, try the totally revamped Infoseek. It has merged four search engines into one integrated tool that's accurate, current, comprehensive, and super fast."

Infospace:
http://www.infospace.com/

InfoSpace helps Internet users find and receive more information in the areas of content, commerce, and community.

Internet Sleuth:
http://www.isleuth.com/gene.html

This site allows you to search up to six genealogy databases on the Web at one time. It contains search links to many genealogy databases.

Linkstar:
http://www.linkstar.com/

The LinkStar Business Directory is one of the Internet's most accurate business-oriented search engines, with more than 320,000 user-entered listings.

Lycos:

http://www.lycos.com/

The heart of the Lycos service is its search engine, which has one of the most complete catalogs of Web site addresses available today. To search for Web sites, enter what you are looking for into the "Search Box" on the Lycos homepage and press the "Go Get It" button. You will then see a list of links to Web pages about your topic.

Magellan:

http://searcher.mckinley.com/searcher.cgi

Magellan offers a unique way to search the Web: by concept. Like most search engines, Magellan is programmed to look for documents containing the exact words you enter into the query box. Magellan goes further and looks for ideas closely linked to the words in your query. This feature can broaden the effectiveness of your search and find more matches.

MetaCrawler:

http://www.metacrawler.com/

MetaCrawler differs from other search services in that it does not maintain its own local database index. Rather, it relies on the databases of other Web-based sources. MetaCrawler sends your queries to several Web search engines, including Lycos, Infoseek, WebCrawler, Excite, Alta Vista, and Yahoo!

Open Text Index:

http://index.opentext.net/

The Open Text Index is a way of finding specific information – words or phrases – on the World Wide Web. You type a word, or a group of words, or a phrase of any length, into a search form. The Open Text Index then searches for occurrences of your search terms and shows you a list of Web pages that include them. It also lets you link to those pages. They index "**every word**" on the entire Web page.

Reference.com:
http://www.reference.com/

Reference.COM makes it easy to find, browse, and search more than 150,000 newsgroups, mailing lists, and Web forums.

Search The Sleuth - Genealogy:
http://www.isleuth.com/gene.html

Searches numerous genealogy sites and databases at once.

Search.com:
http://www.search.com/

SEARCH.COM is a collection of tools designed to find all kinds of information. They also add feature stories to help you find what you're looking for, tutorial help on searching, and a whole lot more.

Starting Point:
http://www.stpt.com/

Starting Point is a search engine and directory site that navigates through Internet clutter intelligently. PowerSearch is a powerful meta searcher with 170 high-quality, popular, and comprehensive search tools, both general and category specific.

webtaxi.com:
http://www.webtaxi.com/

Webtaxi is a navigation service designed to help Internet users conveniently search the World Wide Web. Webtaxi enhances the existing capabilities of current versions of Netscape Navigator. This free service was developed to offer efficient point-and-click access to search engines, newsgroups and thousands of hard-to-reach databases. Webtaxi provides a single interface for searching multiple sites.

What's New Too!:
http://newtoo.manifest.com/

What's New Too! Is a Web announcement service that is a good place to go to keep current on what's happening on the WWW today. It is also a good place to advertise your own Web pages.

Yahoo!:
http://www.yahoo.com/

Yahoo! is a searchable, and browsable hierarchical index of the Internet cataloged by humans. If you know exactly what you're looking for, try using Yahoo! Specify a keyword or keywords, and it will search its entire database to find listings that match them.

Genealogy Graphics Sites

Autumn's Place - Genealogy Graphics:
http://www.aye.net/~autumn/

This site contains some very nice genealogy graphics. Her only limitation is that the graphics can only be used freely on your non-profit USGenWeb, Rootsweb, genealogy, or personal family history site.

Cherished Memories:
http://www.web-trek.net/stern/csindex1.html

A genealogy graphics site by Chris Stern, a graphic artist, beginning genealogist, and former computer technician.

Clip Art and Images by John N. Stewart:
http://desktoppublishing.com/stewart.html

This site has a shareware version of his Antiquities and Antiquities II graphic collections.

Genealogy Clip Art Catalog:
http://www.wwwebit.com/bayberry/geneclip/geneclip.html-ssi

This site has **NO** graphics. It is a catalog for ordering genealogy graphics. All clips are black & white and only in PCX format. The clips are all related to genealogy pursuits and may be useful for newsletters, flyers, reunions, etc.

Genealogy GIFS:
http://www.citynet.net/mostwanted/gengifs/gengifs.htm

This site contains some graphics that may be useful on personal Web pages, and continues to add new graphics regularly. This site also has some genealogy background files as well.

Historical Picture Collections:
http://ac.acusd.edu/History/documents/clipsources.html

This site has links to dozens of sites with selections of all types of historical photographs.

OOGS Genealogy Graphics:
http://home.swbell.net/repa/yoggs.htm

A site with free graphics for the genealogist.

VikiMouse Collection of Genealogy Graphics:
http://www.geocities.com/EnchantedForest/8608/gen.htm

This is a collection of genealogy graphics. These pages are a direct result of a request from Betsy Mills for genealogy graphics. A great many of her ideas have been incorporated here. Within this Web site, there are approximately one thousand graphics.

Vintage Images - Old Fashioned Clip Art:
http://www.wf.net/~jyates/genart.html

This site has a disk for sale with a collection of old-time artwork. They also have a few you can download for free.

E-mail Services

E-Mail Services Home Page:
http://www.usroots.com/

This site is operated by DsEnter.Com. They offer (for a one-time fee of $20) a LIFETIME, "permanent" e-mail address. You will never have to change your e-mail address again, no matter how many times you change your ISP. Your friends and family will only have to remember one e-mail address for you ever again.

Hotmail:
http://www.hotmail.com/

Hotmail is an Internet based, free e-mail provider. They feel that e-mail access should be easy and possible from any computer connected to the World Wide Web.

iName Personalized E-mail:
http://netscape.iname.com/

You can get a Personalized e-mail address at this site. Your Personalized iName can be: @cheerful.com, @scientist.com, @writeme.com, etc. In addition, you'll never change e-mail addresses again. E-mail sent to your permanent iName address is forwarded to your current e-mail account whether it is at home, work, or school. Or you can get an electronic mailbox on iName's server.

Juno:
http://www.juno.com/

Juno provides e-mail service to anyone with access to a personal computer and a modem, and it provides this service at no cost to its members. Their software package runs on PC-compatible computers under Microsoft's Windows® operating system. Juno members do not need to already have any form of Internet access in order to use Juno.

NetAddress:
http://beta.usa.net/

With NetAddress, you'll never again have to change your e-mail address just because you moved or switched to a different ISP. No more informing your friends and family when your e-mail address changes.

Pride Mail:
http://www.pridemail.com/

They offer either a POP or forwarding account for $5.95 a year. You never have to update your e-mail address with anyone but Pride Mail ever again.

How to Turn OFF HTML or RTF in e-mail:
http://www.rootsweb.com/rootsweb/listowners/html-off.htm

Many people have been having problems with red backgrounds and other strange things in e-mail messages. This Web site explains how to turn off the advanced features that cause problems with e-mail.

Travel Services

Expedia:
http://www.expedia.com/

Microsoft's Expedia travel site. You can research, reserve, and buy your travel arrangements online. They have simple step-by-step wizards to make it fast and easy to book flights, hotels, and rental cars. You can also sign up to receive e-mail messages each week with the lowest published fares for up to three places you are interested in traveling to.

Online Scotland:
http://www.ibmpcug.co.uk/~ecs/

On-Line Scotland's Web site offers a dedicated service for traveling in Scotland. This site enables you to look at accommodations in detail, gain competitive quotes on car hire, read about areas of Scotland with associated tours, request flight information, and make your own specific personal requirements. If they have not provided the information you require within their site, please enquire, they will be happy to assist. This site should whet your appetite and encourage you to visit Scotland.

Priceline.com:
http://www.priceline.com/

You name the price you want to pay and Priceline will try to find a major airline willing to release seats on flights where they have unsold space. Tickets can be requested up to six months in advance of departure. For leisure travelers who don't need to fly at a specific time of day or on a specific airline, Priceline is a great new alternative.

Southwest Airlines Home Gate:
http://www.iflyswa.com/

This is the home page of Southwest Airlines on the World Wide Web. They offer ticketless travel available online from this site, as well as airport information about the 52 airports Southwest serves, including gate information and directions to the airport. You can check out the flight schedules Southwest offers from Baltimore to Los Angeles, and all the points in between.

The Travel Channel Online Network:
http://www.travelchannel.com/

The Travel Channel Online Network has the following sections: *Spotlight* (in-depth information on a new destination, event or activity); *Travel Channel Cable Networks* (features programming information, scheduling, special features, and events from The Travel Channel cable networks); *Vacations, Holidays & Getaways* (a resource for planning your next trip); *Travel Facts & Opinion* (travel tips, destination suggestions and hot travel news); *Travel Talk* (you can talk to others about anything and everything related to travel by using their bulletin board, or joining in on a travel related chat); *Photo Gallery* (unusual travel photos from around the world).

Travelocity:
http://www.travelocity.com/

Travelocity provides a convenient way to buy airline tickets, reserve rental cars, and book hotels in more than 70 countries worldwide. They have a fare watcher e-mail service – your electronic eye on low fares. You can ask it to monitor the cost of up to five separate round-trips for you. They also have a Travelocity newsletter that will bring you up to date on new features, articles and travel promotions.

Part IV: Where Do We Go Next?

Where Is the Internet Headed?

This question is one that is impossible to answer with any certainty. From what we have seen in the past few years, we venture to say the Internet will be in almost every home within the next five to ten years. The recent growth of the Internet is comparable to the growth of television in the 1950s. What this means for the genealogist is better (quicker, easier, cheaper) communications and greater access to resources that will benefit us all.

Other methods of accessing the Internet are being developed. These methods use something other than a modem, such as satellite systems and cable companies. Many areas already have pilot programs using these technologies. The increased speed of transmission these technologies bring will move us into an information era. Perhaps then it will be practical to read copies of original records stored on microfilm, CD-ROM, or other storage medium over the Internet.

What Effect Will Internet Growth Have on Genealogy?

The keyword here for genealogists is convenience. Even with only partial catalogs online, genealogists already find it beneficial to check the Internet for records to search at a library, archive, or other repository before they leave home. And making travel reservations to libraries and archives is easier than ever, from programs that watch for discount airfares (like **http://www.expedia.com/**) to lists of restaurants in the area you plan to visit. The need to leave home at all will lessen as the Internet provides more and more access to original genealogical source material online.

As the Internet becomes a household commodity, e-mail and electronic publishing will flourish. What a boon this will be for genealogical societies that publish periodicals. Think of the collating and stapling that won't have to be done. You won't have to worry about postal rates going up, or mail being lost or mangled.

Will the Internet have as much of an impact on genealogists and society as the printing press did centuries ago? In a word, yes.

Appendix A: Choosing an ISP
(Internet Service Provider)

Important Considerations

The quality of your life experience on the Internet will be determined largely by the Internet Service Provider (ISP) you decide to use. Richard and Barbara have horror stories about Internet Service Providers they have used over the last decade.

Here are a few things to consider as you make your decision about which ISP to use:

- Your first priority is that access to the ISP be a local phone call. Do not pay twice: once to your ISP and secondly to the phone company for every minute you are connected to and using the Internet.

- What is your time worth? The increasing popularity of the World Wide Web is causing a world-wide-wait; however, not all traffic jams originate on the Internet. How will you feel about getting a busy signal when trying to connect to your ISP? Or as you wait for the number of people logged on to your server to drop, so you can take your turn downloading a file? Ask questions (such as how many access lines that ISP has, and how many callers their lines can handle) before signing up. In fact, it is a good idea (when possible) to choose an ISP that has two local access phone numbers for your area. If one number is busy, you can try to get online using the other number.

- How much hand holding (help) will you need from your ISP? Some providers have toll-free support numbers open twenty-four hours per day, seven days per week, with a real human to speak to you. Do not sign up for a service that suggests you e-mail questions to them or consult their Web site for help. These methods are not much help if you cannot get online to begin with.

- Beware of ISPs that offer a lower price for limited access (five to ten hours per month). Once you exceed the specified number of hours, they surcharge you from $1.95 to $2.95 per hour. Very few genealogists succeed at controlling their connection time once they discover the treasures on the Internet. Surprise monthly bills of $100 or more are not unknown to subscribers of reduction plans.

- Do you need Internet access from a location other than your home? If you travel, you may want an ISP that has many local access numbers available nationwide.

- Are there hidden charges for large amounts of e-mail? This is important if you plan to subscribe to electronic mail lists with large volumes of messages.

- What Web browser does your ISP allow you to use? What is that ISP's connection software like? Some ISPs use browsers that are not compatible with all Web sites. Not all ISPs allow you to use just any Web browser. If you are familiar with one Web browser program, try to find an ISP that allows you to use that browser so you won't have to learn to use new software.

Most of the hassles genealogists encounter are in getting an account set up with an ISP. This involves configuring your equipment to correctly communicate with your ISP's equipment. Surfing the World Wide Web seems really easy after that.

Internet Service Providers: Local & National

Companies that provide direct connections to the Internet are currently the best value. They typically charge from $9.95 to $21.95 per month for unlimited Internet access time. How long this competitive pricing will last is anyone's guess. Most also offer Web space on their server for you to publish (store) your own information (Web pages) on the Internet. This is called "home page" space.

 The type of account you want to get is called a dial-up IP, or SLIP/PPP account. Do not get a text-only account. This type of account is cheap (free to college students) but provides only text-based (Telnet) access, which restricts you from surfing the Web.

Although commercial providers offer a few items that are available only through their commercial bulletin board service (BBS), there is so much information out on the Internet you likely will not miss what the commercial providers offer only on their BBSes. One disadvantage to subscribing to a commercial provider is that they may have their own proprietary browsers (which are usually not as powerful as Netscape Navigator or Internet Explorer). America OnLine (AOL), one of the most popular commercial bulletin board services, now uses the Internet Explorer Web browser.

The biggest advantage to commercial providers is that it is often much easier to set up a connection to a commercial service. They are experienced at helping beginners get connected. They are also usually better at helping beginners get up to speed on the Information Superhighway with their proprietary chat groups and bulletin board areas devoted to Internet use.

A safe bet would be to check with other Internet users in your area. See if they are satisfied with their local ISP. Make sure they tell you all the pros and cons of using their ISP. Just bring up the question at any genealogical society meeting and stand back. Quite a lively discussion is likely to ensue.

Telnet Access

Telnet access to the Internet is usually offered free of charge by universities to their students, teachers, and administrators. Telnet is okay for e-mail, but such Internet access is only text-based. You cannot get to the World Wide Web. Some universities are beginning to offer Web access to current students. While as a researcher you will occasionally resort to using Telnet, this is not as difficult as it was in the "old" days, thanks to the WWW.

If you need to access a Telnet site on the Internet and don't already have a communications program that does Telnet, add a Telnet program to your personal computer. You can go to a Web site like *Tucows* or *Shareware.com* and download a free version of a Telnet program. If you then configure your browser software to work together with this Telnet program, any time you need to access a Telnet site your Telnet program will automatically pop up. Telnet software opens additional resources on the Internet not available through the **http://** connections of the World Wide Web.

Barbara Says:

The best education you could have about the Internet is to read the following glossary. Slowly read and re-read two or three items in the glossary per day. In less than two months, you'll feel much more confident in any Internet discussion.

Appendix B: Glossary

404 Error: HTTP/1.0 404 Object Not Found. This is a common error message you get when your computer fails to find a specific Web page or file on the Internet. This indicates that the file you were searching for does not exist on that server. You may have typed the URL wrong, the Internet may just be very busy, or the file may have been deleted or moved (such a change of address/location is common on the Internet).

Access Number: The telephone number you dial to connect to your Internet Service Provider to get online.

Address: There are three types of electronic addresses on the Internet: e-mail addresses, IP addresses (See **ISP**), and URLs. These are used to navigate to sites on the Internet or send electronic messages to a site on the Internet.

Address Book: A feature found in some e-mail programs to store names and e-mail addresses. (Called "Nicknames" in Eudora Pro.) This is nice because you don't have to remember complicated e-mail addresses. It is nice to be able to "double-click" on a person's name in your electronic address book to insert their e-mail address in a message you are writing.

America Online: See **AOL**.

Anonymous FTP: Computer sites located around the world storing hundreds of thousands of files which are made available for genealogists (and others) to copy freely. Anonymous FTP can be used to copy software, documents, graphics, and many more types of files to your home computer.

AOL: America OnLine. A commercial bulletin board service that also provides Internet access to its customers.

Archie: A tool to help you locate a specific file somewhere out there on the many FTP sites on the Internet, if (and only if) you know the file's name. With millions of text and program files available, some system was needed to help locate a specific file. Archie is especially helpful if you don't know the name of a computer (or the location on a computer) where the file is stored, but you do know the name of the file you are looking for.

Archive: A file composed of one or more files that have been compressed together into one file. See **PKZIP** or **Stuffit**.

Archive Site: A server on the Internet that has an organized collection of files. These files are usually available to the public for downloading.

ASCII: American Standard Code for Information Interchange (pronounced AS-SKI). Gives the alphabet, numbers, punctuation symbols, and computer control codes (such as the control key) a standard code number. Most personal computers use some form of this code. ASCII makes the exchange of text files and GEDCOM files (GEDCOM files are genealogy data files created by a genealogy database program) possible between genealogists. When you hear the term "ASCII Text File," that means the file has been saved in a generic format—a good way to store files.

Attached File: See **Attachment**.

Attachment: A computer file electronically attached and sent along with an e-mail message.

Bandwidth: The amount of information (text, images, video, sound) which can be sent through an Internet connection. Usually measured in bits-per-second (bps). A full page of text is about 16,000 bits. A fast modem can move approximately 15,000 bits in one second (or nearly a full page of text). Full-motion full-screen video, however, requires about 10,000,000 bits-per-second (depending on compression). Obviously more bandwidth (or better compression) is needed if the Internet is to grow and evolve.

Baud: The speed at which your modem sends or receives information, typically over a telephone line.

BBS: Bulletin Board System. A personal computer connected to one or two phone lines, usually for 24 hours a day. Users call into the BBS and log on with a user ID and password. They can then read and leave messages or download files (text, graphic or software). BBSes are largely being superceded by Web sites. See also **commercial BBS**.

Binary file: A non-text file. Examples would be graphic (.GIF or .JPG) or sound (.WAV or .AU) files.

BMP: Bit-mapped graphics format. This is the standard graphic format for Windows and OS/2 operating environments. These graphic files (.bmp) **cannot** be used on Web pages. Web pages can only handle GIF or JPG graphic file formats.

Bookmark: A way to save the URL of a site you may want to visit again. Called "Favorite Places" in AOL or "Favorites" in Microsoft's Internet Explorer.

Bounce: An e-mail message returned as undeliverable. This happens when you send a message to an address that is no longer good or has been mistyped.

Bulletin Board System: See **BBS**.

bps: **B**its **p**er **s**econd is the speed rating of a modem used to connect your computer to a phone line. The minimum speed that many ISP's allow for your connection is 14,400 bps (14.4 Kbps). Many current modems are rated at 56,000 bps (56 Kbps).

Browser: A program specifically designed to give you access to the multimedia information that exists on server computers on the Internet. It lets you surf the Web. With a browser and an Internet connection you can search and view documents on the World Wide Web that contain text, sound, graphics, and video. A browser allows you to "jump" from one location to another by clicking once with your mouse on highlighted and/or underlined words or graphics called "links." Links can be either words or pictures.

Browser Caching: Because browsers store recently accessed Web pages on the user's computer, users may need to periodically empty these caches. Caching is used by your computer to speed up Internet access to recently visited Web pages. If you find your hard disk suddenly full, it may be because of this caching. You may need to have your browser empty the cache if you are getting low on disk space.

BTW: Commonly used in e-mail to mean: **B**y **T**he **W**ay.

Case Sensitive: Be aware that about 70% of the Internet is on case sensitive computers. If you type in the URL address of **www.Compuology.com** the server may not recognize it as being the same address as **www.compuology.com**. So be aware of the case when typing URLs and e-mail addresses.

CC: **C**arbon **C**opy. To send an additional copy of an e-mail message to someone else by adding their e-mail address in the CC: field.

Chat: See **IRC**.

CIS: See **CompuServe**.

Client: You and your computer are considered the client in the Internet client-server relationship. (See also page 14.)

Commercial BBS: A commercial computer network that provides it's members with proprietary features (such as: Bulletin Board Message areas and chat rooms, for a monthly fee. Examples are AOL, CompuServe, and Prodigy. They also provide Internet access.

Commercial Online Service: See **Commercial BBS**.

Communications program: Software that allows your computer to communicate with other computers, usually over telephone lines, via a modem. They are used less often today because of the advent of Web browsers.

Compression: A method used to reduce the size of a file. Examples of compression programs include PKZip and WinZip. A compressed file takes less time to send over the Internet than a non-compressed file.

CompuServe: A commercial bulletin board service that also provides Internet access.

Congestion: The reason the Internet seems to slow down during times of heavy usage.

Connection: When two computers establish communication for the exchange of information. Commonly used to refer to "going online."

Cookie: A small amount of information stored on your computer by some Web sites you visit. This information is used to let the Web site know about you to speed up your next visit. This file can get quite large and takes up space on your hard drive.

Counter: A system for telling how many people have looked at a Web page. Each access (look) is referred to as a hit.

Cyberspace: Describes any of the information that is available through computer networks, including the Internet.

Dial-up: A connection made to a computer via a telephone call. This requires a modem to change the digital computer signal to an analog signal that can be transmitted over a telephone line.

Digest mode: The grouping of messages recently posted on a mail list so they can be sent as one e-mail message to all of that mail list's subscribers. [Also something you do to the food you eat. :-)]

DNS Entry: **D**omain **N**ame **S**erver. Domain Name Servers are connected to the Internet. They translate the letters in an Internet address into a numerical IP address. It is much easier for most of us to remember www.compuology.com than the corresponding IP address, which is 205.214.171.151, so give thanks for Domain Name Servers.

Domain Name: An exclusive name identifying an Internet (server) site. Domain names have two or more parts separated by periods (called dots). One computer may host more than one domain name, but a specific domain name points to one and only one computer. For example in the address www.compuology.com "compuology" is the domain name and the extension "com" (the domain) indicates that "compuology" is a company. "www" indicates it's a

Web site. In addition to "com," other top level domains are "net" (network), "org" (usually a non-profit organization), "edu" (educational institutions), "gov" (government organizations) and "mil" (military). (See the chart on page 22.)

Domain Name Server: See **DNS Entry**.

Download: The process of copying a file from a computer somewhere on the Internet "down" to your computer.

E-mail: Electronic mail. You have an electronic "address" where you receive your e-mail, and you send e-mail to people at their electronic "address."

E-mail Overload: Being overcome by the amount of e-mail you receive.

Emoticons: One of these :-) (created in this case by typing a colon, a hyphen, then a right parenthesis) or his cousins. A way of expressing emotion in your electronic mail messages via typing.

Encryption: Making a message or file generally unreadable for purposes of privacy. This requires an encryption program.

Error Messages: One common message on the Internet is "Server has no DNS entry." This can be caused by many things. You may not be connected to the Internet when you run your browser, the URL you typed may be incorrect, the server you are trying to connect to may be offline for maintenance, or the Internet is just too busy to give you a connection to the site. (See also **Congestion**).

FAQ: Frequently Asked Questions. Not just the questions, but also a list of answers to those frequently asked questions about a site, service, or a topic.

File Compression: See **Compression**.

File Transfer: See **FTP**.

Flame: A virulent personal attack directed at a mail list or newsgroup participant who did not, in the flamer's opinion, follow the social mores of the subscribing group. Sent via e-mail and posted physically on a mail list or a newsgroup.

Flame-bait: To post an inflammatory statement with the intent of provoking.

Flame War: What happens when a series of inflammatory posts are exchanged rather than useful information in a Usenet newsgroup, Mail List, etc.

Forwarding: Sending an e-mail message you received on to someone else.

Free-net: Free limited Internet access provided to people in a certain geographic area, usually through/at public libraries.

Freeware: Software available openly to the public without a registration fee.

FTP: File Transfer Protocol is a program, as well as a set of procedures or rules, for transferring files from one computer to another via the Internet.

FWIW: Commonly used expression meaning: For What It's Worth.

FYI: Commonly used expression meaning: For Your Information.

\<G\>:   Commonly used in e-mail to mean "**G**rin." Also \<g\>.

GEDCOM: Stands for **GE**nealogical **D**ata **COM**munications. It is the method used to transfer genealogical data between different computer programs. This allows you to move your genealogy data from one software program to another without having to re-type it.

GIF: **G**raphic **I**nterchange **F**ormat (pronounced Jiff , like the peanut butter choosey mothers choose.) A graphic format used on the Internet. This format was introduced by CompuServe for transferring graphics electronically.

Gigabyte: One billion characters. The minimum size your hard drive needs to be to hold all the Internet files you have downloaded. :-(

GIGO: Acronym for "**G**arbage **I**n **G**arbage **O**ut." Meaning the computer is only as good as the person typing the commands.

Gopher: A menu based system developed to help organize text information on computers. It's purpose is to make locating and retrieving information easier. This used to be the primary navigational tool for the Internet. Today search engines for the WWW have replaced much of the need for Gopher.

Handle: Your nickname online.

Hardware: The physical parts that make up your computer.

Header: See **Message Header**.

Hits: The number of times a Web page is loaded (looked at) by a Web Browser. See also **Counter**. Some sites try to figure out how popular they are by counting the number of hits they get.

Home Page: This is the main page of a Web site. Usually it has the filename *index.html*. If you don't designate the HTML page name the program will search for index.html first, then index.htm, etc. If you type the URL **http://www.compuology.com** then the Web page **http://www.compuology.com/index.html** will load.

Host: This refers to the computer (server) where Web pages are located (stored).

Hostname: The name of a computer on the Internet.

Hot Link: See **Hyperlink**.

HTML: **H**yper **T**ext **M**arkup **L**anguage is the language used to write Web pages. It includes (text or graphical) links that send you to another page somewhere else on the World Wide Web when you "click" your mouse on them. This computer language gained fame because it was used to create the World Wide Web.

HTTP: **H**yper**T**ext **T**ransport **P**rotocol tells the computer which language to use in order to look at a document, picture, or site on the Internet.

Hypertext: A document that contains hyperlinks.

Hyperlink(s): This refers to a highlighted and underlined section of text or graphic icon that takes you to another area of the Internet with the "click" of a mouse button.

Icon: A small picture you click on to go somewhere, do something, or start a program.

IE: See **Internet Explorer**.

IMHO: Common expression meaning: **I**n **M**y **H**umble **O**pinion.

Inbox: A folder where your incoming e-mail is placed.

Infobahn: See **Information Superhighway**.

Information Superhighway: Used to mean the Internet or World Wide Web.

Internet: The term "internet" was originally used to describe any network that connected two or more computer networks to each other. Actually, it was called an "internetwork." In theory, any network of networks is an internet (for example, if the five computers in your office are connected to a network of computers at UCLA that is an internet. However, when people talk about "the Internet" what they are referring to is the Internet that spans the globe, connecting individuals, businesses, universities, governments, countries, and continents. The Internet is a vast resource and useful tool for genealogists.

Internet Explorer: Microsoft's Web browser.

InterNIC: Internet Network Information Center. InterNIC describes itself as "a cooperative activity between the National Science Foundation and Network Solutions, Inc. and AT&T." In addition to providing a wide variety of Internet related informational and educational services, InterNIC is the organization that registers domain names and allocates IP numbers.

IP: Internet Protocol address. A numerical Internet address consisting of four sets of numbers separated by dots. (See also **DNS Entry**.)

IRC: Internet Relay Chat. A method of having real-time typed "conversations" with others on the Internet.

ISDN: **I**ntegrated **S**ervices **D**igital **N**etwork uses digital signals to more than double the amount of data that can be sent over a standard phone line. An advantage is that it provides a clean and noise free dial-up connection for transferring information over the Internet. It also allows data and voice transmissions to be transmitted at the same time over one plain copper telephone line, for nearly the same cost as a regular phone call.

ISP: **I**nternet **S**ervice **P**rovider. The company you use to connect to the Internet.

JPG: **J**oint **P**hotographic Experts **G**roup (pronounced J-PEG). A graphic format used on the Internet that reduces the size of images by a factor of 10 or more with little degradation of the image. These files take less space on your Web site, but are slower loading because the receiving computer must un-compress the graphic file to display it

Keyword: Words input into a search engine, or other search field to locate possible matches of those words in the files or documents that are being searched.

Line Noise: Telephone line static that can interfere with data (Internet) transmissions.

Link(s):   An electronic connection between two sites on the Web. See also **Hyperlinks**.

Listserv: A list server is a computer that hosts a mail list you can subscribe to. Some are maintained by robotic programs while others are maintained by a sometimes on vacation (get a real life) human. (Unlike CompuServe there is no **e** at the end of Listserv.)

Logon: To make a connection to any remote computer. The opposite of logoff. <g>

LOL: Expression meaning: Laughing Out Loud.

Lurk: To read newsgroups or mail lists but not post any messages. This is a good thing to do when you first subscribe to a new mail list or newsgroup, until you learn the netiquette of that group.

Lynx: An older text-based Web browser for the Internet.

Mail List: An e-mail address that electronically forwards messages to a list of subscribers. See **listserv**.

Mail Server: A computer on the Internet that provides mail list services.

Majordomo: A program that handles mail lists, much like Listserv.

Megasite: A site, such as Cyndi Howell's, that contains links to hundreds or even thousands of sites on the Internet that relate to a certain topic, like genealogy.

Message Header: Information placed at the beginning of an e-mail message. Headers typically contain information about the sender, receiver, subject and date.

Meta Search Engine: A search engine interface that actually performs a search using many search engines at the same time.

MIME: Multipurpose Internet Mail Extensions. Used to send pictures, formatted word processing files and other non-standard (not ASCII text) files via e-mail.

Modem: The name comes from **MO**dulator/**DEM**odulator, which describes how it works to transmit data to and from your computer. This is the essential device that connects your computer to a telephone line for access to the Internet. Modems are rated in bps (bits-per-second). (See BPS)

Moderator: Someone who reads all the messages posted to a newsgroup or mail list before publicly posting them. The moderator can "kill" messages that are offensive or not related to the topic.

Mosaic: One of the first browsers for the World Wide Web.

Multimedia: Documents containing data in different formats, such as graphics, sounds and video.

Netiquette: The etiquette of the Internet.

Netscape Navigator: Still (perhaps) the most popular Web browser software available for the Internet.

Network: Computers connected together.

Newbie: A new person on the Internet. What you were before you read this book.

Newsgroups: Discussion groups based on a specific topic. Over 30,000 separate newsgroups exist, each group covering a different topic.

Node: Another name for a host computer.

Page: See **Web Page**.

Password: A secret code you need to log onto a computer.

Path: The full description of where a file is located on a computer.

PDF: **P**ortable **D**ocument **F**ormat (PDF) is a method of providing formatted documents over the Web. You will need a special reader program to view the documents—called Adobe Acrobat. (It is available for free at **http://www.adobe.com/acrobat**).

PKZIP: A file compression program. It creates a file that usually ends in the extension *.zip*, that can contain one or more compressed files. The receiver must use a program like PKUNZIP to restore the files to their original state.

POP: Point Of Presence. The access location for an ISP. When your computer dials a telephone number to connect you to the Internet, it is dialing the number of your ISP's local POP.

Posting: An individual e-mail message sent for display on the Internet in a mail list or newsgroup.

PPP: Point-to-Point Protocol allows you to dial in and enjoy nearly the same benefits as if you were working at that computer half way around the world. PPP is considered superior to the older SLIP connection protocol. When looking for an ISP, make sure they provide you with PPP/SLIP access to the Internet.

Prodigy: A commercial bulletin board service.

Protocol: A rule of how computers will act when "talking" to each other. These protocols allow different types of computers with different operating systems to communicate.

Query: A message created to help the genealogists locate distant relatives or researchers of a common ancestor. Generally a query should have an ancestor's name, location where they lived, and the time period they lived there.

Query Terms: Words you type into a search engine that it uses to compare to its list of words from Web sites on the Internet.

Readme File: A text file, included with a program, that explains details for installing and running that program. Often these contain last minute changes to the printed manual.

ROTFL: Commonly used expression, means: **R**olling **O**n **T**he **F**loor **L**aughing.

Search Engine: A tool for looking up information on the Internet
You can search by keywords, phrases, or topics. Each of the popular search engines operates a little differently. You may find something with one search engine that you could not find with another. Search engines search the Web and index what they find. Most are updated every 2 - 3 weeks. Some search engines are better at specific types of searches.

Server: Typically a big computer that provides a service to other computers known as clients. Any computer that is permanently connected to the Internet is a server. They may store and make accessible Web pages, mail lists and/or newsgroups.

Service Provider: See **ISP**

Shareware: Computer programs that you can try before you buy. Often available for downloading from the Internet.

Shouting: SHOUTING IS WHEN YOU TYPE IN ALL CAPITAL LETTERS IN ONLINE COMMUNICATIONS. This is considered bad Netiquette (except for SURNAMES in genealogical areas).

SLIP: **S**erial **L**ine **I**nternet **P**rotocol allows you to dial in and enjoy nearly the same benefits as if you were working at that computer half way around the world. It doesn't contain all the features of PPP and is slower.

Smiley: See **Emoticons**.

SMTP: **S**imple **M**ail **T**ransfer **P**rotocol. The protocol that controls e-mail format and functioning.

Snail Mail: Mail sent through the U.S. Postal Service.

Software: The programs that control how the hardware of your computer operates and make it work for you.

Spam: Unsolicited junk e-mail sent to large numbers of users at a time.

Stage Directions: Used in Internet communications to convey attitudes. Surrounded by <.>, such as <grin>.

Stuffit: A Mac file compression program that creates a file containing one or more compressed files.

Subscribe: To join a group (such as a mail list) or service (such as MSN). There may or may not be a charge depending on the group you join.

Surf: You surf the WWW by clicking on a highlighted or underlined text or graphic, activating a hypertext link, thus connecting (taking) you to different locations.

TCP/IP: Transmission Control Protocol/Internet Protocol. The communications standard that allows different types of computers to communicate with each other (PC's, mini-computers, mainframes, even Mac's.) Yes, the PC and Mac can get along together on the Internet. TCP/IP is the foundation upon which the Internet was built.

Telecommunication: Communicating via a telephone line be it digital or voice signals.

Telnet: In the "old days," you connected to another computer on the Internet by way of a program called Telnet. You typed in commands on a command line (if you knew them and could type them correctly), and Telnet located the other computer and established a connection with it. If you were listed in the remote computer's files as an authorized user, you could "log in" and use the other computer as if your keyboard were connected directly to it. This was all text-based.

Text file: A file in ASCII format, usually ending in the extension *.txt*. This may be the best way to store your word processor files for long term storage. That way even if your word processor program is no longer around you can probably read and use the file with the current software.

Thread: Ongoing messages or answers relating to a message that was previously posted to a newsgroup. Any message can trigger a follow-up message.

TIF: **T**agged **I**mage **F**ile Format. This is a popular graphic file format. It cannot be used on Internet Web pages.

TTYL: Commonly used in e-mail to mean: **T**alk **T**o **Y**ou **L**ater.

Unix: The name of the computer operating system that has served as a foundation for much of the programming behind the Internet. Often found on very large mainframe computers.

Upload: To transfer your files to someone else's computer.

URL: Uniform **R**esource **L**ocator. The electronic address of a document, or Web page, on the Internet. It functions like a "street address," indicating where the document or file is located. These addresses usually will look something like this: **http://www.compuology.com/**

USENET: The thousands of newsgroups together make up something called USENET. Often used interchangeably with the word newsgroup.

User ID: The name you choose when you sign up with an ISP. You need this name and a corresponding password to log onto the system.

Utility: A program that performs a useful function, such as the PKZip compression program. Utility programs can often provide useful features that were left out of major programs.

Uuencode/uudecode: A method for changing non-text files into a format suitable for e-mailing. When received the recipients' software must decode the file back into its original form. An older and cruder method than MIME.

VBG: Commonly used in e-mail to mean: **V**ery **B**ig **G**rin.

Veronica: Similar to Archie. It is built into Gopher to allow you to search all Gopher sites for files, directories, and menued items. It can be useful for searching the text-based portion of the Internet.

Viewer: A program used to look at non-text files. L-View Pro is a typical viewer for viewing graphic files (such as digitized original source records downloaded from a Web site).

VT100:   Many computers on the Internet expect to talk to this type of terminal. Therefore, when Telnetting, if asked for terminal type you should usually select VT100.

WAIS: **W**ide **A**rea **I**nformation **S**ervice. A powerful tool for searching for information in libraries and databases on the Internet.

Web Browser: See **Browser**.

Web Page: This refers to a multimedia document (HTML document) on the Web. They generally end in the extension *htm* or *html*. An example would be **filename.htm** or **filename.html**. Although considered a single Web page, when printed out such a document may be many pages long.

Web Site: A location (server computer) that contains many Web pages.

Webmaster: The person responsible for maintaining a Web site.

WinZip: Windows or Windows 95/98 file compression program. See also **PKZip**.

Wired: Being connected to the Internet.

World Wide Web: See **WWW**.

WWW: World Wide Web. A system that can handle multimedia functions over the Internet. Also known as "The Web". It is made up of two parts: browser software that can "read" or "view" multimedia documents (files) and server computers that can support and maintain multimedia documents. The Internet and the World Wide Web are not separate entities. The computers that store and make available Web documents are part of the Internet network.

Zip file: A file that has been compressed with either the PKZip or WinZip programs. This makes the file smaller and it then takes less time to send over the Internet.

Index

1990 Census 133
20th Century Direct 106
411 Directories 26, 146
555-1212.com 146
AAA Map'n'Go 149
Acadian 72
ACPL 98
Adjacency 54
Adobe Acrobat 190
Advanced search 53, 54, 56-59
Advertising 52
African American 70, 72
Afrigeneas 72
AGI - Chat Room 144
AGLL 106
Aid Association for Lutherans 74
ALA 98
Albion 67
All-in-One Genealogy Search Page 49, 114, 152
All-in-One Search Page 57
Allen County Public Library 98, 126
Alpha software 88
Alta Vista 11, 52, 53, 56, 152
Amazon Books 106
America OnLine 173
American Directory Assistance 146
American Genealogical Lending Library 106
American history 72
American Library Association 98
American Life Histories 114
American ships' lists 122
Ancestors 131
Ancestors Found! 64
Ancestral Quest 83, 86
Ancestry 106

Ancestry Research Site 114
Ancestry World Tree 114
AniMap 89
Ann Turner's GEDCOM Utilities 83
Anonymous FTP 46
AOL 173, 177, 179, 181
APG 90
Appleton's Books 107
Archer, George 135
Archie 48, 178
Archived files 56
Archives and Manuscripts Database 123
Archives Web 115
ArchivesUSA 115
Arkansas 124, 127
ARPAnet 5
ASCII 178, 189, 194
Asia 70
Ask Quailind 131
Association of Professional Genealogists 90
AT&T 187
Augustana College Library 74
Australia 70, 78, 94
Automated Research 107
Autumn's Place 158
Bancroft Library 116
Banner Blue 85
Beard, R. 11
Best Websites for Helping Genealogists 68
Bible records 123
Big C 143
Bigfoot 146
Biography.com 115
Birth Year Calculator 131
BLM Land Patent Search Site 115
Board for Certification of Genealogists 90, 138
Book Craftsman 107
Bookmarks 51, 52, 179

Books We Own Project 116
Bookstores 67, 77
Boolean operators 54
Bounced e-mail 30
Bradford, William 123
Brigham Young University 98
British Columbia 116
British Columbia Archives 116
British surnames 119
Brøderbund Software 121
Broken Arrow Publishing 107, 139
Browsing 16, 21, 49, 50, 57, 67, 149
Bureau of Land Management 115
Byron Sistler and Associates 107
BYU 98
Cadillac 13
Calendar 64, 66, 69, 131
Calendar Creator 131
Calendar of Genealogical Events 64
Calendars of Genealogical Events 12
California Academic Libraries List of Serials 101
California Genealogical Society 90
California Heritage Collection 116
California Heritage Digital Image Access Project ... 116
California Historical Society 90
California State Genealogical Alliance 91
California USGenWeb Archives 117
Canada 23, 67, 70, 94, 102, 109, 112, 116, 124, 147
Canadian 72, 92, 102, 120, 126
Canadian Geographical Names 102
Capital Community-Technical College 142
Cardiganshire 80
Carl Sandburg College 132
Carlsbad Library 94
CARLweb 98
Carmarthenshire 80
Carpatho-Rusyn Knowledge Base 76
Case Sensitive 180

Case sensitivity 54
CD Lookups 138
CD-ROM 109
Cemetery Listing Association 117
Census - Lookups 132
Census Indexes 133
Census Project 129
Census View 108
Center for Life Stories Preservation 132
CGSSD 91
Chance's Genealogy 68
Channel Islands 80
Chat Page 144
Chat Room 144
Chat Sessions 42
Cherished Memories 158
Cherokee 72, 124
Cherokee National Historical Society 72
Church of Jesus Christ of Latter-day Saints 99
Church of the Brethren 73
Citing Online Sources 142
Citing Sources & Writing Skills 142
Civil War 72-74, 109, 117
Civil War Battle Summaries 73
Civil War Soldiers & Sailors System 117
CLA 117
Clark County, Nevada Marriage Inquiry System 118
CleanSweep 150
Clearfield Company 108
Client-server relationship 15
Clip Art and Images 158
Collabra 39
Collins, Ron 137
Commsoft 89
Compuology . . . . iv, v, 63, 64, 66, 94-97, 117, 180, 182, 186, 194
CompuServe 70, 181
Computer Genealogy Society of San Diego 91
Computer virus 14

Confederate Pension 118
Connecticut 102
Cool Site of the Month for Genealogists 64
Cooley, Michael 69
Copyright 45
Copyright Basics 143
Copyright Information 143
Copyright Myths 143
Corel Family Tree 83, 84
County Finder 132
Cousin Finder 128
CPCGN 102
Crawlers 52
Cross, William D. 57
CSGA 91
Cumberland Family Tree 83
Cyndi's List 50, 68
Czech Info Center 76
Czech Republic 76
DALnet 145
Database of Irish On-Line Resources 76
Dataviz 25, 149
Daughters of the American Revolution 94
DBI-LINK 76
Dead People Server 73
Dear Emily Postnews 67
Death Master File 114
DeLorme On-line Store 149
Design Software 84
Dictionaries 11, 13, 70, 81, 82, 101, 132, 137
Dictionaries & Etc 81
Digest mode 32, 182
Digital Digest 112
Directories 26, 50, 59, 130, 146, 147, 195
District of Columbia 94
Division of Library Automation 101
DLA 101
Domain name 22, 25, 33, 182, 183

DOS 4, 46, 83, 149
Drudge, Bob 70, 103, 142
Dutch 82, 122, 125
E-mail 22, 23, 25, 40, 174, 183, 184
E-mail attachment 25
E-mail Services 160
E-mail Software 22
E-ttachment opener 25, 149
EarthLink 25
East Tennessee Historical Society 91
Eastman, Dick 81
Eastman, Richard 112
Eastman's Online Genealogy Newsletter 112
Education and Training 9
Electric Library 99
Electronic publishing 168
Ellen Payne Odom Genealogy Library 112
England 79, 80
English 11
Eppstein, David 86
Eppstein, Diana 86
Ethics 90
Ethnic and Special Interest Sites 72
Etiquette 43, 67, 190
Eudora 24, 177
Eudora Light 24
Eudora Pro 24, 35
Europe 57, 70, 89, 140
EuroSeek 152
Events 7, 12, 31, 64, 66, 69, 98, 100, 112, 163
Everton Publisher 108, 118
Exchange 35
Excite 56, 152
Expedia 10, 162
Extension 22, 63
Family Census Research 84
Family Chronicle 65, 108, 119
Family Forest 84

Family Forum 65
Family Gathering 89
Family Heritage 83, 84
Family Heritage Deluxe 84
Family histories 66, 90, 109, 133
Family History Center 70, 135
Family History Information 135
Family History Library 99, 134
Family Marriage Research 84
Family Matters 84
Family Origins 84
Family Photo Historian 132
Family Tracker 85
Family Tree House 85
Family Tree Maker 85, 119, 141, 143, 153
Family Tree Online 112
FamilyFinder Index 119
FamilySearch 86
FAQs 143
Favorite Places 179
Favorites 179
Federal Census Indexes 133
Federation of East European Family History Societies 51, 77, 92
Federation of Family History Societies 92
Federation of Genealogical Societies 92, 117
FEEFHS 51, 77, 92
FFHS 92
FGS 92
File attachments 24
File Transfer Protocol 44, 184
Filez 153
Finding People 7
Findspot 153
Flags Of The World 73
Flamed 43
Flyte Comm 11
Foreign 8, 11, 76
Foreign Genealogy Sites 76

France 94
Free Agent 40
French 36, 72, 78, 82, 126, 144
Frequently Occurring Names 133
Frontier Press 108
FTP 6, 44-47, 65, 111, 133, 140, 143, 153, 177, 178, 184
Fuller, John 145
Funeral Net 119
Gary Kemper's German Resources 77
Gateway Press 109
Gazetteer 78, 102, 104
Gazetteer for Scotland 102
GED-BOOK 86
GEDCOM 24, 25, 86, 88, 119-121, 130, 178
GEDCOM Utilities Page 86
GEDUTILS 83
GEDWRAP 83
GEN-BOOK 86
GEN-WEB Site 119
GENCMP-L@MAIL.EWORLD.COM 33
GenConnect 120
GENDEX 120
Gene 86
Genealogical and Historical Societies 90
Genealogical Cemetery Database 84
Genealogical events 64
Genealogical GEDCOM Server System 121
Genealogical Helper 108, 118
Genealogical Jamboree 96
Genealogical Products and Supplies 13
Genealogical Publishing Company 108
Genealogical Society of Utah 117
Genealogical Software Sites 83
Genealogical Websites of Societies & CIGS 92
Genealogist's Index to the World Wide Web 120
Genealogy 133
Genealogy and Poland 77
Genealogy Anonymous FTP site 140

Genealogy Articles & Files 133
Genealogy Book Stores & Publishers 106
Genealogy Books 109
Genealogy Bulletin 106
Genealogy Channels 145
Genealogy Classes 132
Genealogy Clip Art Catalog 158
Genealogy Databases @ Internets 120
Genealogy Databases @ Internets 120
Genealogy Dictionary 81, 133
Genealogy Exchange & Surname Registry 121
Genealogy Gateway 68
Genealogy GIFS 158
Genealogy Graphics Sites 158
Genealogy Helplist 133
Genealogy Home Page 65
Genealogy Launch Pad 134
Genealogy Mall 109
Genealogy Megasites 68
Genealogy Online 69
Genealogy Queries 123
Genealogy Related Newsgroups 144
Genealogy Resource Page 134
Genealogy Resources on the Internet 65
Genealogy Search Engine 153
Genealogy Software Springboard 87
Genealogy Tools & Training 131
GenealogyLibrary.com 121
Genealogy's Most Wanted 134
General Genealogy Sites 64
Generations 87
GenForum 144
GenSearcher 49, 114, 152
GENSERV 121
GENTECH 93
GenWeb Project 96
GenWeb.Net 66
Geographic extensions 23

Geographic Names Information System 105
Georgia 104, 112
German Genealogy 78
German Libraries 76
German resources 77
German Translation Service 81
Germans from Russia Heritage Society 77
Germany 109
Gittings, Bruce 102
Glamorgan 80
GMW Chat Page 144
GNIS 105
Gold Bug 89
Gooldy, Pat 111
Gooldy, Ray 111
Gopher 48, 99, 195
Government CD-ROMs 109
GPO 109
Graphical interface 24
Graphics 44, 45, 47, 56, 158, 159, 177, 179, 180, 185, 190
Grassi, J. Ron 145
Great Britain 109
Gressa, Greg 76, 81
Guide to Grammar and Spelling 142
GWSC 92
Haliburton, J. Peter 145
Handle 24, 46, 144, 171, 179, 185, 196
Hargrett Library 104
Headers 32, 37, 189
Hearthstone Bookshop 110
Helm's Genealogy Toolbox 69
Heritage Genealogy Software 87
Heritage Quest 106
Hierarchy 50, 144
HiJaak 150
Hispanic 70
Historical County Lines 103
Historical Ink 102

Historical Picture Collections 159
Hoffman, Gary B. 143
Hoosier Genealogist 113
Horus 139
Host 27-29, 31, 37, 40, 45, 66, 96, 152, 182, 186, 190
HotBot 53, 55, 56, 153
Hotmail 160
How to Turn OFF HTML or RTF in e-mail 161
Howell, Cyndi 50, 189
HTTP 44
Hughes, Anthony 142
Hypertext links 21
HYTELNET 99
I Found It! 153
IAF 146
Iberian Publishing Company 109, 110
ICONnect 134
Illinois 122, 132
Illinois Land Records 122
iName Personalized E-mail 160
Index to Passenger Lists 122
Indiana Historical Society 113
Information about Copyrights 143
Information Superhighway 5, 6, 14, 187
Infoseek 154
Infospace 154
Institute of Genealogy & Historical Research 138
International Internet Genealogical Society 93
International Internet Genealogical Society University 141
Internet Address Finder 26, 146
Internet directory service 26
Internet Explorer . 16, 21, 24, 38, 39, 44, 51, 122, 173, 179, 186, 187
Internet FamilyFinder 153
Internet Genealogical Directory 144
Internet Public Library 99
Internet publication 143
Internet Relay Chat 145
Internet resources 63

Internet Search Tools 152
Internet Service Provider 15, 22, 24, 26, 171
Internet Sleuth 154
IRC 145, 187
Ireland 80, 109
Irish Family History Foundation 94
Isle of Man 80
ISP 15, 16, 51, 161, 171, 173, 180, 188, 191
Italian 78
Italian Genealogical Group 78
Janyce's Root Diggin' 69
Japan 94
Jewish 70
Jewish Genealogy 74
JewishGen 74
Journal of Online Genealogy 113
Juno 160
Kemp, Thomas J. 68
Kemper, Gary 77
Kentucky Death Index 122
Kessler, Louis 88
Keyword 17, 30, 34, 35, 40, 43, 50, 52-55, 57, 157, 168, 188
Keywords 40, 48, 53, 56, 59, 149, 157, 192
Kindred Konnections 122
Kingwood College Library 142
Kinpublish 87
Kinwrite 87
KINWRITE Plus 87
KY Biographies Project 128
L-View Pro 195
Lacy's Genealogy Gateway 123
Land terminology 12
Language Aids 11, 81
Latin 11
Lawson McGhee Library 91
LDS . . . . v, 70, 99, 111, 134, 135
LDS Church 135
Legacy Family Tree 87

Lester Productions 87
Library & Catalog Sites 98
Library and Archives Resources 70
Library of Congress 47, 100
Library of Virginia 9, 46, 100, 123
Lineages 123
Lineages Genealogy Queries 135
Links 21, 188
Linkstar 154
List Servers 145
LISTSERV@MAIL.EWORLD.COM 33
Locating Living People 146
Locating Societies 12
Logon 37, 46, 188
Los Angeles Public Library 4, 100
Louis Kessler's Genealogical Program 88
Louisiana 127
Lutheran Roots 74
Luxembourg Gazetteer 78
Lycos 52, 56, 155
Lynx 189
Macintosh . . . . ix, 5, 16, 45, 46, 85-88, 149, 151
Macintosh Genealogy Programs 88
Magazines . . . . v, 49, 77, 99, 106, 142
Magellan 155
Mail list 28, 32
Mail Lists 25, 27, 34, 37, 43, 145, 189, 191, 192
Mail Lists, Newsgroups, & Chat Sites 144
Mailbox 30
Maine 102
Manuscript Database 123
Map & Gazetteer Sites 102
MapBlast! 10, 103
MapQuest 10, 103
Maps and Cartography 103
Massachusetts 102
Master Genealogist 89
Mavrogeorge, Brian 68

Mayer, Alicia P. 95
Mayflower 127
Mayflower Passenger List 123
McAfee 149
Medical Resources 13
Megasites 49, 59, 68
MELVYL 101
MetaCrawler 155
Mexico 94
Microfilm Catalogs 110
Microsoft Network 25
Microsoft Word 86
Mills, Betsy 159
MIME 195
Mindscape 84
Mining Company 69
Missouri 75
Molineaux Diary 74
Moobasi 107
Mormon Pioneers 140
Mount, Jack 103
MSN 25
Murphy, Jeff 128
Murphy's Law 51
Murray, Sabina J. 140
My Virtual Reference Desk 70, 103, 142
My-ged.com Server 124
Myer, Rex 130
NAIL 124
Naming Traditions 136
NARA 124, 135
National Adoption Registry, Inc. 147
National Archives 110, 115, 131, 138
National Archives Records Administration 124
National Genealogical Society 93, 136
National Park Service 73
National Science Foundation 5, 187
National Society Daughters of the American Revolution 94

National Society Sons of the American Revolution 94
National Union Catalog of Manuscript Collections 136
Natural language 56
NAVA 74
NEHGS 93
NetAddress 161
NetGuide - Genealogists Guide to the Internet 135
Netiquette 33, 43, 67, 190, 192
Netiquette Home Page 67
Netscape 21, 46, 63, 130
Netscape Communicator 39, 51
Netscape Mail 35
Netscape Navigator 16, 21, 38, 39, 173, 190
Network Solutions, Inc. 187
New England Historic Genealogical Society 93
New Hampshire 102
New Jerusalem 135
New South Wales Registry 78
New York 102
New Zealand 70
Newsgroup 40, 184, 191, 194
Newsgroups 29, 36, 37, 40, 43, 56, 189, 192
Newsgroups on the Internet 145
Newspapers 77, 99, 100, 113, 116
NewsRover 40, 149
NGS 93
Nickname 22, 35, 43, 144, 185
Nicknames 136, 177
NIDS 115
North American Vexillological Association 74
North Carolina 107, 134
North Dakota 77
North San Diego County Genealogy Society 94
Northern Ireland 94
Norton Anti Virus 150
Notable Women Ancestors 75
Nova Scotia 122
NSDAR 94

NSDCGS 94
NSFNET 5
NSSAR 94
NUCMC 115, 136
Obituaries 31, 109, 113, 120, 123, 124, 152
Obituary Daily Times 124
OCCGS 95
Occupations Descriptions 137
OCLC 101
Oil Change 150
Old Disease Names 137
Old German Script 81
Old Parish Registers 79
OLIVE TREE Genealogy Homepage 125
On-line Books 125
OneLook Dictionaries 11, 81, 137
Online Bible Records 125
Online Catalog 125
Online Computer Library Center 101
Online Databases for Genealogists 114
Online Dictionaries and Translators 82
Online English Grammar 142
Online Genealogical Database Index 125
Online Genealogy Publications 112
Online Grammars 82
Online Pioneers 110
Online Resources for Writers 142
Online Scotland 162
Online Telephone Directories 147
OOGS Genealogy Graphics 159
Open Text Index 155
Orange County California Genealogical Society 95
Origins of Family Names 137
Other Computer Software Sites 149
Other Genealogy Sites 65
Our Ancestors Nicknames 138
Our Family Tree 88
Outlook 35

Outlook Express 24, 35, 39
PAF 83, 86-88
PAF Review 88
Passenger lists 109, 122, 125
Password 46, 179, 190, 195
PC Computing 154
PC Magazine 8
PC Webopaedia 11
PCL Map Collection 104
Pembrokeshire 80
Pennsylvania 122
People Search USA 147
PERiodical Source Index 126
Perry-Castaneda Library 104
PERSI 126
Peterson, Paul 68
Phrase 17, 54, 56, 57, 125, 155
Phrases 54
PKZip 25, 178, 181, 191, 195, 196
Poland 10, 51, 77, 79, 103
Polish 11
Political Graveyard 75
Pony Express 75
Priceline.com 162
Pride Mail 161
PRO 79
Procomm Plus 150
Prodigy 181, 191
Prohibited terms 55
Proximity 54
Proximus 104
Public Record Office 79
Publishers 77, 106, 110, 118
Publishing 66, 95, 107, 108, 110, 111, 139, 168
Quarterdeck 57
Quarterdeck Corporation 150
Questing Heirs Genealogical Society 95
Ramsey, JGM 91

Rand Genealogy Club 95, 138
Rankings 55
Rare Map Collection 104
Reference.com 156
Remick, Bruce 68
Repeat Performance 138
Repositories of Primary Sources 126
Required terms 55
Research 8
Research Tools 138
Reunion 87, 88
Reverse Area Code Directory 147
Reverse Look Up Directory 147
Rhode Island 102
Richard Eastman's Genealogy Forum 70
Richard Wilson's Home Page 66
Richard's "Other Genealogy Web Sites 66
Ridenour, Carla 112
Ridenour, Dennis 112
Rigdon, John 120
RLIN AMC file 136
Robots 52
Roots Surname List 126
Roots V 89
Roots-L 35, 116, 126, 127
RootsWeb 127
Rootsweb Mailing List Archives 127
Royal Scottish Geographical Society 102
RSL 126
Russia 109
Salt Lake City 140
Samford Institute 138
San Diego Genealogical Society 95
Santa Barbara Genealogical Society 95
SBCGS 95
SCCAPG 96
SCGS 96
Schulze, Lorine McGinnis 125

Scotland 79, 80, 109, 162
Scots Origins 79
Scott McGee's GenWeb Page 127
Scottish Resources 80
Scottish Roots 79
Scrapbooks 106
Search International 147
Search The Sleuth 156
Search.com 156
Searchable Genealogy Links 70
Searching 57
Seeker Magazine 148
Shareware 24, 42, 46, 84, 86-88, 150, 153, 158, 174, 192
Ship lists 122
Silicon Valley PAF Users Group 96
Sistler, Byron 107
SMITH, Patience Lowery 35
Smolenyak, Megan 76
Snail mail address 25, 134
Soc.genealogy 37, 144
Social Interaction 14
Social Security Death Index 114, 128
Social Security Index 118
Software 9
Sons of the American Revolution 94
Soundex 120, 138
South & West Wales Genealogical Index 80
South Carolina 127
South Dakota 127
South Orange County California Genealogy Society 96
Southern California Chapter, APG 96
Southern California Genealogical Society 96
Southern families 128
Southwest Airlines 163
Special Home Pages 145
Spectrum Virtual University 139
Spiders 52, 56
Spiders' Apprentice 58

SpryNet/CompuServe 46
St. Clair, Mike 64, 92
Starship Enterprise 17
Starting Point 156
Stern, Chris 158
Stewart, John N. 158
Street Atlas USA 149
Subscribe 28-30, 39, 172, 188, 189, 193
SupportHelp.com 150
Surfing 57
Surfing vs. Searching the Internet 48
Surname Genealogy Web Project 139
Surname Origin List 119
Surname Registry 121, 139
Surnames 139
SurnameWeb 139
Sutro Library 131
SVPUG 96
Switchboard 148
Switchboard Directory 26
Telnet 3, 4, 45, 47, 100, 174
Tennessee 12, 49, 91, 107, 127
Texas 71, 93, 101, 104, 118
Texas Internet Consulting 70, 71
Texas State Archives 118
Texas State Electronic Library 101
The Computerized Ancestor 111
The Family Tree 112
The Global Gazette 112
The USGenWeb Project 129
The Weather Channel 11
THOMAS, Adonijah 35
Thread 38, 194
TIC 71
TIGER Mapping Service 104
TMG 89
TN-Roots 35
Tombstone Transcription Project 128

Top Ten Genealogy Websites Nominees 65
Tracing Mormon Pioneers 140
Tracing your Scottish Ancestry 80
Traffic jams 171
Travel Channel 163
Travel Help 10
Travel Services 162
Traveller Southern Families 128
Travelocity 10, 163
Travlang's Translating Dictionaries 82
Treasure Maps 140
TripQuest 103
Tucows 151, 174
Turner, Ann 83
Twenty Ways to Avoid Genealogical Grief 140
U.S. Gazetteer 104
U.S. Geological Survey 105
U.S. Government 3, 109, 143
U.S. Government Printing Office 109
U.S. Surname Distribution 105
U.S. territorial expansion 103
UC union catalog 101
UK and Ireland 80
Ultimate Family Tree 89
United Daughters of the Confederacy 117
United Kingdom 23, 79, 94
United States Internet Genealogical Society 97
University of Arizona Library 58, 103
University of California 101
University of California, Riverside 139
University of Edinburgh 102
University of Georgia Library 104
University of Illinois 122
University of Texas 104
URL 31, 39, 47, 48, 177, 179, 180, 183, 186, 194
US Biographies Project 128
US Land & Property Research 141
US Postal Service 148, 193

Usenet 36, 56, 127, 143, 149, 152, 184, 194
User ID 179, 195
User login name 25
USGenWeb Archives 117, 129
USGenWeb Archives Search Engine 129
USGenWeb Project 117, 130, 143
USGS 105
USIGS 97
Utah 97, 99, 117, 140
Utah Valley PAF Users Group 97
UV-PAF-UG 97
VA-Roots 35
Vermont 102, 127
Veronica 48, 195
Veteran and Military Web Sites 130
Vexillology 73
Viewer 46, 195
VikiMouse Collection 159
Vintage Images 159
Virginia 9, 46, 100, 107, 111, 118, 122, 123
Virtua-Web 125
Virus Hoax Site 151
Virus hoaxes 145
Virus, computer 14
Vital Records Information 141
WAGS 97
WAIS 99, 195
Wales 79, 80, 109
Washington, George 54
WDC 130
WDC GenWeb Project 130
Web Browser 195
Web Browsers 21, 44, 45
Web of On-line Dictionaries 11, 82
WebBoard 128
webCATS 101
WebCompass 57, 150
Webcrawler 56

WebGene 130
Webified Genealogy 130
webtaxi.com 156
What's New Too! 157
What's in a Name? 139
What's New Too! 157
What's Really New in WWW Genealogy Pages 49, 66
Where to Write for Vital Records 141
Whew! 35, 151
Whittier Area Genealogy Society 97
Who Owns Genealogy? 143
Wholly Genes, Inc. 89
WhoWhere? 26, 148
Wildcards 55
WILLISON, Isaac 31
Willow Bend Books 111
WILSON 31
WILSON, Micajah 35
Wilson, Richard S. 64
WILSON-L@rootsweb.com 31
Win-Family Home Page 89
Winch, Randy 86
Windows 5, 149, 151, 179, 196
Windows 3.x 46
Windows 95/98 .... ix, 16, 25, 46, 83, 151, 196
WinZip 25, 181, 196
Wisconsin 127
WORD 97 34
Word/Phrase Search 125
WordCruncher 35, 151
WordPerfect 86
WordPerfect 8 34
World Descendant Charts 130
World Genealogy Web Project 130
World GenWeb Project 130
World Wide Web 4, 6, 45, 52, 171, 172, 186, 190
Worms 52
WPA Project 114

Writing 142, 177
WS_FTP 46
WWII U.S. Veterans Web Site 75
Yahoo! 50, 52, 71, 157
Yates Publishing 111
Ye Olde Genealogie Shoppe 111
Zarahemla Book Shop 111
Zip 25, 104, 148, 191, 196
Zip Code 104, 148
Zip Code Information 148
ZUCKNICK 51